# ONE IN
# CHRIST

## BIBLICAL CONCEPTS FOR A DOCTRINE OF CHURCH UNITY

## DENIS FORTIN

 **Pacific Press®**
Publishing Association

Nampa, Idaho | Oshawa, Ontario, Canada
www.pacificpress.com

Cover design by Steve Lanto
Cover design resources from Lars Justinen

The author assumes full responsibility for the accuracy of all facts and quotations as cited in this book.

Unless otherwise noted, all Scripture quotations are taken from the New King James Version®. Copyright © 1982 by Thomas Nelson. Used by permission. All rights reserved.

Scripture quotations marked NASB are taken from the NEW AMERICAN STANDARD BIBLE®, copyright © 1960, 1962, 1963, 1968, 1971, 1972, 1973, 1975, 1977, 1995 by the Lockman Foundation. Used by permission. www.lockman.org.

Scripture quotations marked NIV® are from THE HOLY BIBLE, NEW INTERNATIONAL VERSION®. Copyright © 1973, 1978, 1984, 2011 by Biblica, Inc.® Used by permission. All rights reserved worldwide.

Additional copies of this book are available for purchase by calling toll-free 1-800-765-6955 or by visiting http://www.AdventistBookCenter.com.

ISBN 978-0-8163-6351-3

April 2018

# Dedication

I am indebted to
Doug, Lorelei, Michael, and Ann,
who through their patient example and good words
unknowingly taught me much about God's family.

# Contents

# Introduction

The church is God's family on earth, serving humanity and worshiping together to the glory of God. Looking to Jesus as its leader and redeemer, the church is called to take the good news of salvation to all people (Matthew 28:19, 20). The Seventh-day Adventist statement of fundamental belief on the church states in part: "The church is the community of believers who confess Jesus Christ as Lord and Saviour. In continuity with the people of God in Old Testament times, we are called out from the world; and we join together for worship, for fellowship, for instruction in the Word, for the celebration of the Lord's Supper, for service to humanity, and for the worldwide proclamation of the gospel."[1]

But what do we mean by church? Who is a part of the church? The answers to these questions depend in part on our definition of the church and who is a child of God.

By church we often refer to the building in which Christians assemble. But this definition falls short because the church is about people, not buildings. A church is the local community of believers who assemble for worship. They can meet in humble homes or in grand cathedrals, but the place of assembly is not the determining factor in one's status as a child of God or inclusion with the community of believers.

In the New Testament, the church is sometimes referred to as the group of believers in a particular geographical area. When Paul addressed a letter to the church in Galatia, he referred to many local congregations in towns and villages of that region (Galatians 1:2) and Peter did the same in his first epistle (1 Peter 1:1). By church, we can also mean a group of people who belong to a particular denomination or who call themselves by a particular name—the Seventh-day Adventist Church, the Baptist Church, or the Methodist Church.

Yet, all these definitions are incomplete if we do not include another key concept. The church is the people of God who believe in Jesus—regardless of the particular name by which they call themselves. We believe the church is composed of all believers whom Jesus died for (Ephesians 5:25) and who accept Jesus as their Savior. The church is equivalent to God's family. Paul stated in Romans 10 that whoever claims to be a follower of Jesus ought to be accepted as such. "The Scripture says, 'Whoever believes on Him will not be put to shame.' For there is no distinction between Jew and Greek, for the same Lord over all is rich to all who call upon Him. For 'whoever calls on the name of the LORD shall be saved' " (Romans 10:11–13).

However, the church, whether we speak of its expression in local congregations, in denominational groups, or in the universal family of God, is hardly a united body of believers. Human sinfulness has limited our ability to live in unity. So is unity possible? What do we mean by church unity?

Adventist professor G. Arthur Keough stated, "Many Christians talk about unity, but few know what they are really talking about. Most people will admit that unity in the church is desirable, but not many can tell you how to achieve this goal. Is it organizational and administrative unity that is needed? or is it unity of doctrine and teaching? or is it some kind of spiritual unity?"[2]

Officially, Seventh-day Adventists believe in church unity within our own denomination and for the entire family of God. Our fundamental belief titled Unity in the Body of Christ states,

# Introduction

The church is one body with many members, called from every nation, kindred, tongue, and people. In Christ we are a new creation; distinctions of race, culture, learning, and nationality, and differences between high and low, rich and poor, male and female, must not be divisive among us. We are all equal in Christ, who by one Spirit has bonded us into one fellowship with Him and with one another; we are to serve and be served without partiality or reservation. Through the revelation of Jesus Christ in the Scriptures we share the same faith and hope, and reach out in one witness to all. This unity has its source in the oneness of the triune God, who has adopted us as His children. (Ps. 133:1; Matt. 28:19, 20; John 17:20-23; Acts 17:26, 27; Rom. 12:4, 5; 1 Cor. 12:12-14; 2 Cor. 5:16, 17; Gal. 3:27-29; Eph. 2:13-16; 4:3-6, 11-16; Col. 3:10-15.)[3]

The source of church unity is the oneness of the triune God and is found in a common bond to Christ. Our relationship with God in Christ is an invitation to live the unity we have in Christ by the sanctifying power of the Holy Spirit. This unity is a divine attribute and an apostolic value as taught by Jesus and the apostles (John 17; Ephesians 4:3).[4]

The subject of unity is timely because Christian believers face countless challenges to their unity in Christ. Turning to the Bible, they find insight and instruction on how to live God's gift of oneness in Christ. In these pages, we will search for concepts on which to build a strong foundation for the doctrine of Church unity.

---

1. "Our Beliefs: The Church," Adventist.org, https://www.adventist.org/en/beliefs/church/the-church/.

2. G. Arthur Keough, *Our Church Today* (Nashville, TN: Review and Herald®, 1980), 70.

3. "Our Beliefs: Unity in the Body of Christ," Adventist.org, https://www.adventist.org/en/beliefs/church/unity-in-the-body-of-christ/.

4. Graham A. Cole, *He Who Gives Life: The Doctrine of the Holy Spirit* (Wheaton, IL: Crossway Books, 2007), 241.

# CHAPTER 1

# God's Original Plan

The biblical story of God's people begins with the creation of earth and humanity. At the end of the sixth day of Creation, Genesis declares that "God saw everything that He had made, and indeed it was very good" (Genesis 1:31). Complete harmony reigned between nature and humanity—as God had intended it. His original purpose in creation included the harmonious coexistence of all life-forms, and He made the beautiful world just for the human family. Everything was perfect. The original world was one of harmony, unity, and love.

Any attempt to understand the nature of unity in the church begins with an awareness of God's original plan at Creation, the unfortunate Fall, and the need for restoration. The first chapters of the Bible show that God desired for humanity to remain one family. Sadly, they also record the roots of disunity and division. Sin derailed God's ideal plan, and the plan of salvation seeks to restore it. This restoration and the unity of all God's people is the ultimate goal of God's love.

### One family in God's image
The book of Genesis says God created humankind in His image. "Then God said, 'Let Us make man in Our image, according to Our likeness. . . .' So God created man in His

own image; in the image of God He created him; male and female He created them" (Genesis 1:26, 27). Although theologians have debated for centuries the exact nature of this image, and the nature of God, many passages of Scripture present God's essential nature as loving and merciful (1 John 4:7, 8; Exodus 34:6), characteristics that can exist only in relationship with others. Our Creator is clearly a God of relationships.

During the week of Creation, God created two institutions that reveal the original desire for the unity of the human family, both centered on human relationships. When Adam and Eve were united to form the first human family, their union had a clear purpose: to become one flesh. The Hebrew word in this expression is used elsewhere to refer to God's nature (see Deuteronomy 6:4) and underlines the intrinsic unity of this relationship.

God's original purpose is also reflected in the institution of the Sabbath as a day of rest. From the beginning, the Sabbath was intended for all humanity (Mark 2:27, 28). Six hundred years before Jesus, the prophet Isaiah highlighted the universality of the Sabbath and its benefits for foreigners and eunuchs, people who were at that time excluded from Israel (see Isaiah 56:1–12). Yet Sabbath and its observance were intended for more than the people of Israel. It was a day of rest designed to remind the descendants of Adam and Eve of their common bond to God and one another. The family unit, also instituted in Eden, forever linked the Sabbath, family, and relationships. More than on any other day, Sabbath fellowship is a foretaste of the life God intended at Creation. It is a preview of the earth made new (see Isaiah 65:17, 21–25; 66:22, 23).

### The consequences of the Fall
However, the beautiful world God created with such care and attention was marred by sin and the enormous consequences of the Fall. Adam and Eve's disobedience fractured the harmonious interdependence between all life-forms and plunged humanity into disunity, discord, and division. On the first day of their transgression they blamed each other for what had

happened and indirectly blamed God (Genesis 3:12, 13).

Over time, this disobedience spawned a tragic course of events that affected all of God's creation. The natural world began to suffer, and human relationships soon followed. Cain and Abel, two brothers who should have loved and cared for each other, became alienated when one wished to follow his own selfish inclinations instead of God's prescribed mode of worship. This estrangement resulted in violence and death. Cain's reaction, however, was primarily against God, not his brother. He felt angry toward God (Genesis 4:5), and this led to resentment toward Abel.

After a few generations, human life degenerated into conflict, violence, and disgrace. Things became so bad God repented of having created human life and wished to destroy it before it worsened. "Then the LORD saw that the wickedness of man was great in the earth, and that every intent of the thoughts of his heart was only evil continually. And the LORD was sorry that He had made man on the earth, and He was grieved in His heart" (Genesis 6:5, 6). The consequences of the Fall progressively degraded God's entire creation. In mercy and justice, He had no other choice but to destroy the antediluvians, saving a remnant so the plan of salvation could be realized for the entire human race.

After the Flood, God established Noah as a kind of second Adam and gave him and his family a promise. The rainbow in the sky would always be a reminder of His care and promises, His kindness and mercy (Genesis 9:12–17; Isaiah 54:7–10). He instituted a covenant with Noah and, in an act of re-creation, launched His plan to have a united and faithful human family.

After the Flood, the plan quickly went awry with the construction of the Tower of Babel. The descendants of Noah who settled in the land of Shinar (Genesis 11:2), today's southern Iraq, soon forgot the God of Noah and the promises He had made to never again destroy the world by a flood. Building the Tower of Babel was a monument to their superior wisdom and skills. Their desire to "make a name for ourselves" (verse 4), secure independence from God, and indulge self-sufficiency were their core motives for this building project. It was also an attempt at circumventing another possible flood and betrayed their supreme distrust of God's promise to never again destroy the earth by water (Genesis 9:8–17).

God's response to this defiant act was to confuse their communication. Up to this point, humankind had spoken one language and shared one culture, but the rebellious tower caused God to confuse the languages of the people and set off a dispersion. The Hebrew play on words in this narrative is instructive—God confuses (*balal*) their language as they construct their Tower of Babel (*babel*) (Genesis 11:9). The fall of Adam and Eve began the sad saga of human disunity, and post-Flood events further eroded the unity of the human race and God's original plan. The Tower of Babel and the subsequent confusion of languages resulted in many people groups who have been at odds, if not at war, ever since.

Thankfully, God's plan of salvation was not foiled because He found someone among these confused people who had kept the true faith, with whom He could restore His covenant and prepare the way for the Messiah and the reunification of the human family. The transition from the confusion in Babel (Babylon) to the calling of Abraham is important: Abraham is called out of Ur, a prominent city in the land of Shinar. God directly disavows the culture from which Abraham came and chooses to begin again in the land of Canaan (Genesis 11:28–12:6).

### Abraham, father of God's people

The three great monotheistic world religions, Judaism, Christianity, and Islam, look to Abraham as their father. He stands in the unique position of being the father of all believers in these three traditions. For Christians, this association is a spiritual relationship. When called to leave his country in Mesopotamia, Abraham was told that in him "all the families of the earth shall be blessed" (Genesis 12:3; see also Genesis 18:18; 22:18; 26:4; 28:14). While God initially chooses one man and his family, His final objective is to reach all humanity with His grace and blessings. Thus, Abraham is the father of God's people, and his trust in God is at the core of biblical unity. The success of God's covenant with humanity hinges on this faith relationship. God works through people to restore unity and to make His will known to lost humankind.

Hebrews 11:8–19 gives three important elements of Abraham's faith, elements that are central to unity among God's people. The first element is obedience to God's will. "By faith Abraham obeyed when he was called to go out to the place which he would receive as an inheritance. And he went out, not knowing where he was going" (verse 8). A second element is hope in the promises of God. "By faith he dwelt in the land of promise as in a foreign country, dwelling in tents with Isaac and Jacob, the heirs with him of the same promise; for he waited for the city which has foundations, whose builder and maker is God" (verses 9, 10).

The third element is trust in God's plan of salvation. The greatest test to Abraham's faith came when God asked him to sacrifice Isaac on Mount Moriah (Genesis 22:1–19; Hebrews 11:17–19). In spite of conflicted feelings and perhaps even against his better judgment, Abraham complied with the request to sacrifice his son, trusting in God's promises. This is why the Old Testament describes Abraham as a friend of God (2 Chronicles 20:7; Isaiah 41:8) and the New Testament says that his faith justified him (Romans 4:1–3). Such faith and trust also built an amazing relationship between God and Abraham. "The pain and agony felt by Abraham at the prospect of sacrificing Isaac in some small way helps us understand the suffering of the Father when he offered up his Son for us all."[1] His life of faith, his unwavering obedience, and his confidence in God's promises serve as an example for the church of today. As modern Christians live these same elements of Abraham's life, they create a common bond of unity. Christian unity rests on the twin realities of a faithful God and a faithful life.

## God's chosen people

In calling Abraham to be His servant and father a vast nation, God chose his descendants to represent Him to the world. It was an election and calling born of God's love and grace. In his review of God's blessings to Israel, at the end of their sojourn in the wilderness, Moses reminded Israel of this call: "For you are a holy people to the LORD your God; the LORD your God has chosen you to be a people for Himself, a special treasure above all the peoples on the face of the earth. The LORD did not set His love on you nor choose you because you were more in number than any other people, for you were the least of all peoples; but because the LORD loves you, and because He would keep the oath which He swore to your fathers, the LORD had brought you out with a mighty hand, and redeemed you from the house of bondage, from the hand of Pharaoh king of Egypt" (Deuteronomy 7:6–8).

God's love for humankind stands at the center of Israel's election as His people. He made a covenant with Abraham and his posterity to preserve the knowledge of God and bring about the redemption of humanity (Psalm 67:2). Yet, it was a supreme act of love that caused Him to choose Abraham and the children of Israel. The heirs of this calling, both literal and spiritual, have nothing to boast about save God's unmerited love.

In a strange reversal of values, God rejects conventional human wisdom when He selects His people. While humans value wisdom, power, and self-confidence when choosing leaders, God passes over the strong and mighty, choosing those who sense their weakness, folly, and nothingness—making it clear there is no room for boasting in God's presence (1 Corinthians 1:26–31).

In Hebrews 11, the faithful from Abel to Abraham met with God's approval. They are shining examples of the principle that faith in God is the decisive factor in godly living. By faith, they saw the promise of a new earth from afar. They lived for the fulfillment of that promise and focused their lives on their eternal inheritance. Though in the world and subject to temptation and deception, their hope was steadfast, their pilgrimage undaunted by the transient nature of the present life. From afar, they saw the new inheritance, and lived in the hope of a better life and a more permanent home.

The lives of these faith heroes are examples for modern Christians. "Therefore we also, since we are surrounded by so great a cloud of witnesses, let us lay aside every weight, and the sin which so easily ensnares us, and let us run with endurance the race that is set before us, looking unto Jesus, the author and finisher of our faith" (Hebrews 12:1, 2).

God's original plan at Creation called for a harmonious and unified human family. The disobedience of Adam and Eve interrupted this plan, but in Abraham He established a people through whom He could keep the promise of restoration alive. Today, no less than long ago, unity remains an essential element of God's plan of salvation in Christ.

----

1. H. M. Wolf, "Abraham," in *Evangelical Dictionary of Theology*, ed. Walter A. Elwell (Grand Rapids, MI: Baker Book House, 1984), 7.

# Causes of Disunity

Old Testament prophets such as Jeremiah, Hosea, Amos, and Micah repeatedly called on the people of Israel to obey God's instructions rather than follow their own inclinations. But the temptations were great, and soon after the conquest of Canaan, the Israelites found themselves attracted to the Canaanites' gods. Repeated warnings against such attraction were ignored, disobedience grew, and disregard for God's Word led to increased apostasy and disunity.

Obedience to God's laws was designed to preserve God's people from the natural and tragic consequences of sin, setting them apart as an example to the surrounding foreign nations. Following God's will would create harmony and strengthen their community against the inroads of evil worship practices. God intended His people to be a holy nation and a witness to the nations (Deuteronomy 7:1–8). To be such a witness, however, the Israelites needed to be united in their common purpose to give glory to God.

Unfortunately, Israel's story is quite different from what God planned for it. In bold relief, Israel's history shows the causes of disunity among God's people and serves as a lesson book for today's believers. Their mistakes and the fatal consequences are no less threatening today. Our unity is under attack, and Satan would like nothing more than to thwart God's purpose for His church as it prepares for Jesus' second coming.

### Doing their own thing

The history of Israel is filled with disobedience and anarchy, followed by a return to God and obedience, then followed again with more disobedience and conflict. This pattern repeats itself over the centuries. Each time the Israelites consciously followed His will, they were blessed with peace and prosperity. Each time they disobeyed and followed their own way, their lives became miserable, often filled with war and conflict. Even before Israel entered into the Promised Land, God predicted this pattern and through Moses offered the solution to avoid such a tortured existence. God desired their undivided love and devotion (see Deuteronomy 28:1–68).

Such commitment proved difficult to maintain, and the book of Judges records numerous accounts of the Israelites ignoring the Lord's will for their lives. Soon after they entered Canaan, people began to pattern their spirituality after the false religions of the surrounding Canaanites. Their unfaithfulness is shocking: "Then the children of Israel did evil in the sight of the LORD, and served the Baals; and they forsook the LORD God of their fathers, who had brought them out of the land of Egypt; and they followed other gods from among the gods of the people who were all around them, and they bowed down to them; and they provoked the LORD to anger. They forsook the LORD and served Baal and the Ashtoreths" (Judges 2:11–13). A key indicator of the frayed religious and social conditions of the day is this line from the book of Judges: "In those days there was no king in Israel; everyone did what was right in his own eyes" (Judges 17:6; also 21:25).

In the words of Ellen White, this apostasy reflected directly on the character of God and God's plan for His people.

> The Lord had through Moses set before His people the result of unfaithfulness. By refusing to keep His covenant, they would cut themselves off from the life of God,

and His blessing could not come upon them. At times these warnings were heeded, and rich blessings were bestowed upon the Jewish nation and through them upon surrounding peoples. But more often in their history they forgot God and lost sight of their high privilege as His representatives. They robbed Him of the service He required of them, and they robbed their fellow men of religious guidance and a holy example. . . . Their covetousness and greed caused them to be despised even by the heathen. Thus the Gentile world was given occasion to misinterpret the character of God and the laws of His kingdom.[1]

In contrast to these stories is the example of Ruth, a young Moabite woman who had married a man from Bethlehem. In the time of the Judges, she is a beacon of spiritual light and devotion in a sea of apostasy and unfaithfulness. After losing her husband, her mother-in-law, Naomi, urged her to stay in her homeland and remarry. But Ruth would have none of it.

"Entreat me not to leave you,
Or to turn back from following after you;
For wherever you go, I will go;
And wherever you lodge, I will lodge;
Your people shall be my people,
And your God, my God.
Where you die, I will die,
And there will I be buried.
The LORD do so to me, and more also,
If anything but death parts you and me" (Ruth 1:16, 17).

What a contrast between the general spiritual apathy in Israel and that of Ruth. Her confession of faith to Naomi is one of the most precious witnesses of trust in God in all of Scripture. "Without a doubt, Ruth's loyal love for Naomi is one of the strongest themes flowing through this story—a love that in the end will prove more extraordinary and selfless than anyone could guess."[2]

What a blessing it is to see that in the midst of anarchy and spiritual declension, God has faithful people who desire to serve Him with all their hearts. Undoubtedly, it is this kind of love and devotion that will bring unity among His people.

## Foolish counsel

While Ruth's story is inspirational, the sad tale of King Rehoboam is not. Son of King Solomon, his reign showcases the tragic consequences of an unwise decision to impose more conscripted labor on his people after the temple in Jerusalem was completed (1 Kings 12:1–24). Admirably, he sought counsel from two groups of advisors, but his final decision to follow the counsel of less-experienced young men brought tragedy to the eighty-year-old monarchy built by David and Solomon. The young counselors advised the king to intimidate the crowd by declaring that he was tougher than his father had been. It was foolish counsel, but the young advisors believed that concession to the people's demands for less rigorous labor was not the leadership style suited for a king. Rehoboam should instead be ruthless and cruel. In the end, he showed just that, becoming a bully underserving of his people's allegiance and faithfulness.

How easy it is to destroy in a matter of days what has taken a lifetime of hard work and dedication to build. S. J. DeVries notes that "possibly this passage's most important lesson is how much easier it is to break up what belongs together than it is to restore what is broken."[3] Unity is easily destroyed when leadership fails to consider the long term effects of its decisions.

Ellen White's insights into this story are enlightening:

> Had Rehoboam and his inexperienced counselors understood the divine will concerning Israel, they would have listened to the request of the people for decided reforms in the administration of the government. But in the hour of opportunity that came to them during the meeting in Shechem, they failed to reason from cause to effect, and thus forever weakened

their influence over a large number of the people. Their expressed determination to perpetuate and add to the oppression introduced during Solomon's reign was in direct conflict with God's plan for Israel, and gave the people ample occasion to doubt the sincerity of their motives. In this unwise and unfeeling attempt to exercise power, the king and his chosen counselors revealed the pride of position and authority.[4]

This tragic tale is instructive. Disunity is often the result of poor leadership and hewing to poor advice. Lack of foresight, focus on short-term goals, disconnection with the people, and pride are all weaknesses in church leadership that impact church unity. While we readily admit that no one is perfect, leaders often bear the responsibility for making poor decisions that affect the unity of God's people.

Such a scenario can be avoided in our own church communities if we realize that the church belongs to all of its people, not just the leaders. The involvement of the community of believers at all levels of church organization is crucial. From the local congregation to the regional bodies that have oversight of larger geographical areas, members of the community must seek to avoid human elements that negatively affect unity. Leadership is a weighty responsibility, but God promises wisdom to those who seek it: "The fear of the LORD is the beginning of wisdom, and the knowledge of the Holy One is understanding" (Proverbs 9:10; see also Proverbs 4:1–9).

## Schism in Corinth

Turning to the New Testament, we find more examples of disunity among God's people. It seems that human nature is pervasively bent toward selfishness and acting independently— dangerous character traits that destroy God's work. Of all Paul's epistles, the first letter to the Corinthians is most focused on the subject of church unity and the issues that were dividing this new Christian community. Someone from the household of Chloe, likely a leader of a house church in

Corinth (1 Corinthians 1:11), shared with Paul the issues that had developed in their midst. Here is the long list:

- factions and divisions among the believers on the basis of who baptized whom (chapters 1–3)
- an immoral situation among the Corinthians: a young man married his father's wife (chapter 5)
- lawsuits between believers (chapter 6)
- confusion about marriage, celibacy, and divorce (chapter 7)
- disputes over what to eat from the market when animals are sacrificed to idols (chapters 8, 9)
- chaos and confusion in worship services (chapters 11, 14)
- confusion over the use and misuse of spiritual gifts (chapters 12–14)
- confusion about what happens after death and whether there will be a resurrection, and what this resurrection will be like (chapter 15)

The first four chapters of the epistle are an appeal for unity, and the first problem Paul addresses is their division and personal quarrels. From what we read in 1 Corinthians 1:10–17, it appears the Corinthians were arguing about whose teaching was superior or more faithful to Scripture. The believers were divided into camps according to those who had instructed them in the faith. Their division was over interpretation and whose understanding should prevail. Some followed Paul, others Apollos, and still others Peter. There was even a group that followed Christ—which appears to be Paul's tongue-in-cheek rebuke to a group of believers who did not seem to understand that they were also a cause of the schism.

Of course, these factions were a blatant and unfortunate form of cultic loyalty to a strong personality. Later in the epistle (1 Corinthians 3:5–15), Paul emphasizes that each of the leaders they professed to follow were servants of God, doing God's work. Paul, Apollos, and Peter are not to be the cause of division among them. Each apostle had a task to fulfill for the

Corinthians; all were servants of God to His glory, not their own. Paul's overriding concern was the preservation of church unity.

Paul's solution to schism is simple yet requires courage to implement. He reminds the Corinthians that Christians are called to follow Christ, not human beings, however talented or gifted they might be. While these early believers seem to have divided themselves along "party" lines, the apostle stated unequivocally that such divisiveness was not according to God's will. He asserts that Christian unity is centered on Christ and His sacrifice on the cross (1 Corinthians 1:13). Thus, Christian unity finds its source in the worship of one Lord, Jesus Christ. At the foot of the cross, all people stand on the same level ground. Baptism is into Jesus, who alone can cleanse from sin. These realities fuel the believer's faith and are cause for celebration. Paul cautions the Corinthians about the wisdom of the world, the dangers of boasting, and their need to refocus their faith on Jesus.

There are four thoughts he shares in the first two chapters to cure division produced by personality cults.

*First Corinthians 1:17*—Paul rejects the values of mesmerizing speakers who draw glory to themselves. All glory is to be given to God, not to human beings. Paul did not preach the gospel in Corinth to attract attention or begin a religious movement in his name.

*Verses 22, 23*—To those hoping for something impressive and irrefutable, Paul preaches the altogether odd and unexpected: Christ crucified. Some Jews were expecting a Messiah who would destroy their enemies and set up a glorious kingdom on earth. Jesus' crucifixion was a stumbling block for them. He did not meet their expectations, so they rejected Him as the Messiah. On the other hand, the Greeks had a worldview that disallowed the idea of God becoming human to redeem humanity. Such a belief for them was foolishness and stupidity. But for Paul, who met Jesus and experienced the results of His ministry, Jesus was the solution to all human woe.

*Verses 30, 31*—For Paul, only God deserves praise. Because

of Christ's death on the cross, Christians benefit from three new realities: (1) righteousness—they are justified and forgiven; (2) holiness—they are set apart for service to God; and (3) redemption—they are free from slavery and sin. These new realities shape their life as a community for God's kingdom.

*First Corinthians 2:1, 2*—Any practical ills and problems in the church are remedied by refocusing on the Cross. Christ crucified is more than just forgiveness and salvation. It is a beacon that lights the way for Christian life and ministry.

Seventh-day Adventists, along with all other Christian groups, cannot afford to take their unity of faith and mission for granted. Like the church in Corinth, today's church can experience division and quarreling that undermines its unity. Paul's timeless words offer a cure to the disease of disunity and internal strife. Only the love and lordship of Christ can transcend dispute and division.

### "Wolves will come"

During his ministry, Paul often faced opposition and knew it would be difficult to preserve the purity of the gospel of Jesus Christ after he was gone. In his farewell to the Ephesian elders in Acts 20:17–38, he drew from the watchman analogy in Ezekiel 33:1–6 to exhort his friends to assume responsibility for safeguarding the gospel. They were to be faithful shepherds of their congregations. Paul's use of the expression "savage wolves" to describe false teachers (Acts 20:29) is reminiscent of Jesus' similar warning that false teachers would disguise themselves in sheep's clothing (Matthew 7:15). Soon after Paul spoke this warning, false teachers did arise and preyed on believers in the Asian churches he had established.

In other epistles, Paul offers additional warnings to the churches of Asia Minor regarding the possible causes of disunity. In Ephesians he mentions "empty words" (Ephesians 5:6) and "fellowship with the unfruitful works of darkness" (verse 11). In Colossians, he refers to "philosophy and empty deceit" and "the tradition of men" (Colossians 2:8). In 2 Timothy, he also warns his friend and colleague, Timothy, who is responsible for the church at Ephesus, against evil behaviors and errors in the church and godlessness in the last days (2 Timothy 3:1–9).

Addressing Timothy's predicament, Paul's recommendation is twofold. First, Timothy should seek God's approval and avoid the shame of disapproval by "rightly dividing the word of truth" (2 Timothy 2:15). The antidote to disputes over useless words and speculation is to correctly understand and teach the Word of God. The truths of the Bible must be rightly interpreted so that no part of Scripture is set in opposition to the entire picture presented in the Bible and to prevent misinterpretations that cause a loss of faith in Jesus. Secondary issues should be subordinated to the principles of God's Word, a word that enables believers to live victorious Christian lives.

Paul's second recommendation is for Timothy to "shun profane and idle babblings" (verse 16). Trivial and speculative topics are not to be part of a faithful and worthy minister's teaching ministry. Trifling and abstract conversations lead only to more ungodliness and do not edify the faith of believers. Truth alone leads to godliness and harmony in the church. The reason Timothy urges people to avoid such errors is that they can easily sweep through the church like a plague or a disease (verse 17). In the end, a firm reliance on teaching the Word of God is the antidote to false teaching and the threat of disunity (2 Timothy 3:14–17).

The Bible, written for our instruction, offers many examples of situations that led to disunity. On each occasion, elements of human nature that generate division among God's people include selfishness, self-interest, love of power, and disrespect for God's Word. Human nature is deceitful above all things and naturally leads to a focus on self and disunity. Awareness of this natural, yet sinful, human tendency is the first step in preserving unity among God's people.

---

1. Ellen G. White, *Prophets and Kings* (Mountain View, CA: Pacific Press®, 1943), 20, 21.

2. Carolyn Custis James, *The Gospel of Ruth: Loving God Enough to Break the*

*Rules* (Grand Rapids, MI: Zondervan, 2008), 48.

3. Quoted in Paul R. House, *1, 2 Kings*, The New American Commentary, vol. 8 (Nashville, TN: Broadman & Holman, 1995), 182.

4. White, *Prophets and Kings*, 90.

# CHAPTER 3

# "That They All May Be One"

The Gospel of John opens a window into Jesus' immediate concerns as His ministry neared its climax. In five crucial chapters (13 to 17) His last words of instruction culminate with His high-priestly prayer (John 17:1–26). A sixteenth-century Lutheran theologian is cited as the first to describe the prayer with this expression. "It is a fitting designation, for our Lord in this prayer consecrates himself for the sacrifice in which he is simultaneously both priest and victim. At the same time it is a prayer of consecration on behalf of those for whom the sacrifice is offered—the disciples who were present in the upper room and those who would subsequently come to faith through their testimony."[1]

The high-priestly prayer is divided into three parts. First, Jesus prays for Himself (verses 1–5), then for His disciples (verses 6–19), and finally for those who would later believe (verses 20–26). At the core of this prayer is Jesus' concern for unity among His disciples and subsequent believers. No meaningful discussion of church unity, of our oneness in Christ, can be complete without giving careful attention to this prayer.

At the beginning, Jesus states that eternal life consists in the knowledge of God. "And this is eternal life, that they may know You, the only true God, and Jesus Christ whom You have sent" (verse 3). Eternal life is realized through a personal relationship with the Father. To know God is not a reference to a simple knowledge about facts (the Greek concept); it means living in fellowship with God (the Hebrew perspective). Such knowledge is deeper and more fulfilling, bringing salvation and eternal life. In this regard, Jesus' incarnation was for the purpose of revealing to humanity a more meaningful and saving knowledge of God. That God, Jesus says, is "the only true God"—a reference to the Hebrew profession of faith in the *Shema*, "Hear, O Israel: The LORD our God, the LORD is one!" (Deuteronomy 6:4). Such knowledge, leading to a meaningful relationship with God, is the true source of unity among God's people.

### Jesus prays for His disciples

Next, Jesus prays for His disciples, a group of men and women He has come to love and appreciate. They are in grave danger of losing their faith in Him in the days ahead, and He commits them to the care of His Father.

His prayer is for their protection in the world. He does not pray for the world because He knows it is intrinsically opposed to the will of the Father (1 John 5:19). However, since the world is where the disciples will serve, Jesus prays that they will be preserved from evil in that world. Of course, He is concerned for the world and, indeed, is the Savior of the world (John 4:4), but the salvation of the world depends on the witness of those who will go and preach the gospel. That is why He intercedes on their behalf, praying that evil will not defeat them (Matthew 6:13).

Knowing that envy and jealousy could divide the disciples, as it had done before, Jesus prays for their unity. "Holy Father, keep through Your name those whom You have given Me, that they may be one as We are" (John 17:11). Perhaps He feared that after His departure the disciples would act on their personal preferences and jealousies, pulling further apart from each other. His burden in these last hours before His death is their unity. Such unity is beyond human accomplishment and can only be the result and gift of divine grace. Their unity, grounded in the unity of the Father and Son, is an indispensable prerequisite for effective service in the future.

Of additional importance for effective service was their sanctification, or consecration in the truth. To this end, Jesus also prays that they be sanctified by the truth, the word of God (verse 17). The work of God's grace on the disciples' hearts will transform them if they allow it. This is critical to the disciples' mission in the world (verse 18). Their service must be "ultimately grounded in divine revelation and predicated on an accurate understanding of and response to such revelation."[2]

### Jesus prays for future believers

After Jesus prayed for His disciples, He broadened His prayer to include future believers. "Jesus' concern for his followers' unity is his greatest burden as his earthly mission draws to a close."[3] "I do not pray for these alone, but also for those who will believe in Me through their word; that they all may be one, as You, Father, are in Me, and I in You; that they also may be one in Us, that the world may believe that You sent me" (verses 20, 21).

Jesus' prayer is a challenge to all church communities today and to the larger Christian community. We live in a world of division and conflict that has sadly found footing in the church family. Few communities of faith are spared this threat of division and disunity. Peter Leithart suggests that Jesus' prayer for unity in John 17:21 "is what Jesus *wants* for his church." However, "it is *not* what his church is . . . [because] visible society is divided, and that means the *church* is divided. This is not as it should be. This is not the church that Jesus desires."[4]

Yet, in spite of Christianity's obvious divisions, Jesus' last wish is a resonating call to Christian unity. There is no doubt that the unity He has in mind is visible unity—"that the world may believe that You sent Me" (verse 21). The world cannot see what is invisible, and those who diminish the importance of church unity must quarrel with Jesus' prayer. He clearly pleads for the Father to establish a visible unity among His followers so that the world may believe in His mission. He prays that the unity of His followers "will have both vertical and horizontal dimensions: vertically, a oneness in the relationship between Christ-followers and the Father and Son . . . ; horizontally, a unity in the relationships between Christ-followers themselves."[5]

What kind of unity does Jesus have in mind? For many people, Christian unity focuses on discussions about organizational unity. However, the unity Jesus refers to "is not organizational, where everyone must be forced into the same denomination. . . . The unity for which Jesus prayed is a unity patterned on the unity of the Father and the Son."[6] J. Marcellus Kik, former associate editor of *Christianity Today*, gives four insights into the meaning of this unity.[7]

First, it is obviously a unity similar to the harmony between the Father and the Son—"as you, Father, are in Me, and I in You" (verse 21). In a few places in the Gospel of John, Jesus referred to the unity of the Father and Son. They never act independently of each other but are always united in everything they do (John 5:20–23). They share a common love for fallen humanity that caused the Father to willingly sacrifice His Son, and the Son complied (John 3:16; 10:15). To know one is to know the other (John 14:7, 9).

Second, it is also a unity in beliefs and doctrine. Jesus insisted that His teachings were in harmony with the Father's will—"My doctrine is not Mine, but His who sent Me" (John 7:16). He also stated, "I speak to the world those things which I heard from Him [the Father]. . . . [A]s My Father taught Me, I speak these things" (John 8:26, 28). Jesus maintained that His teachings were identical to those of the Father. Hence, the unity He speaks of is obviously one that will consider the teachings of Scripture and not promote a relativist understanding of the Christian message. The Scripture is the revelation of the word of God and is to be the basis of all unity.

Third, Jesus refers to a unity in purpose. Jesus claimed that His mission was the mission the Father had given Him in carrying out the work of redemption. They were of one purpose. "For I have come down from heaven, not to do My own will, but the will of Him who sent Me. . . . And this is the will of Him who sent Me, that everyone who sees the Son and believes in Him may have everlasting life" (John 6:38, 40). The will of the Father was the salvation of humanity through the sacrifice of Christ on the cross. The church must echo that same purpose by proclaiming the message of redemption to all humanity.

Fourth, this is a unity in love. "By this all will know that you are My disciples, if you have love for one another" (John 13:35). Manifesting this unity in love will give public confirmation of a genuine fellowship with Jesus and the Father. "The display of their genuine unity ought to provide a compelling witness to the truth of the gospel."[8] This is how humankind will know Jesus is the Savior of the world. In other words, this unity Jesus prayed for cannot be invisible. How can the world be convinced of the truthfulness of the gospel if it cannot see love and unity among God's people?

Jesus' command to love one another (John 13:34, 35) was not a new idea and can be found in the instructions God gave Moses (Leviticus 19:18). What is new is Jesus' command for His disciples to love one another *as Jesus has loved them*. Jesus' example of self-sacrificing love is the new ethic for the Christian community. Love for one another as Jesus loved us is the greatest principle of Christian unity. In a later chapter, we will study how to live this love principle in the midst of conflict and disagreement.

John also spoke about love being the evidence of unity. "By this we know that we love the children of God, when we love God and keep His commandments. For this is the love of God, that we keep His commandments. And His commandments are not burdensome" (1 John 5:2, 3). Generally, while people in society today wish to call themselves law-abiding citizens, it often happens that the same people will downplay the biblical obligation to keep the commandments of God. In reality, many people refuse to submit to God's will because they do not wish to lose their personal freedom, even claiming that God's grace does away with God's commandments. However, that is not the biblical teaching on the commandments of God.

Jesus reminded believers of an enduring principle, "If you love Me, keep My commandments. . . . He who has My commandments and keeps them, it is he who loves Me" (John 14:15, 21). Ekkehardt Mueller observes that "keeping the commandments is not a condition for knowing God but a sign that we know God/Jesus and love Him. Therefore, knowledge of God is not just theoretical knowledge but leads to action."[9]

In 1876, Ellen White gave this significant interpretation of Jesus' words in her testimonies to Seventh-day Adventists:

> God is leading out a people to stand in perfect unity upon the platform of eternal truth. . . . God designs that His people should all come into the unity of the faith. The prayer of the Christ just prior to His crucifixion was that His disciples might be one, even as He was one with the Father, that the world might believe that the Father had sent Him. This most touching and wonderful prayer reaches down the ages, even to our day; for His words were: "Neither pray I for these alone, but for them also which shall believe on Me through their word."
>
> How earnestly should the professed followers of Christ seek to answer this prayer in their lives.[10]

## Unity among Christians

Seventh-day Adventists usually understand Jesus' prayer in John 17 as directly applying to unity within their church denomination and, to a lesser degree, the unity of Christianity as a whole. Of course, Adventists must be united in order to fulfill their mission to share the three angels' messages to the world, but it is also clear that this prayer of Jesus is for all Christianity. He was praying for the future unity of *all* Christians who claim Him as their Savior.

The modern ecumenical movement has embraced this prayer and adopted Jesus' last wish as the inspiration for Christian unity. Yet, this goal of visible unity among all Christians remains elusive. The relationship between various groups of

Christians is complex, and the history of doctrinal and eccle-
sial division goes back centuries. Memories of persecutions and
doctrinal conflicts are difficult to heal; the emotional pain is
deep and beyond human attempts at reconciliation. Like many
other groups, Eastern Orthodox Christians have tried to
understand other Christian churches and how they should
relate to those who do not share their convictions. A simple
statement expresses their understanding of the complexity of
Christian relationships: "The Church is us, but we're not 100
percent sure about the rest of you."[11] It's possible this expression also reflects what many Seventh-day Adventists quietly
think about Christians of other denominations and churches.

Surprisingly, it appears that Jesus' disciples were not sure
about other people who also claimed to be followers of Jesus
and yet were not part of their inner group of disciples. In
Mark 9, after the Transfiguration, Jesus and three of His disciples (Peter, James, and John) are faced with a scene of demon
possession (Mark 9:14–29). The other disciples had been unable
to help this father and his son. Whereupon, Jesus casts out the
demon from the young boy and returns him healthy to his
father.

Shortly thereafter, having arrived in Capernaum, Jesus asks
the disciples what they had been discussing between themselves
on the road (verses 33–37). It turns out they had been quibbling
about who was the greatest. So to illustrate what discipleship is
really about, Jesus takes a little child and states that "whoever
receives one of these little children in My name receives Me"
(verse 37)—a statement that in itself broadens the definition of
who is a disciple of Jesus. And that broadened definition looks
like this—a disciple of Jesus is a child who may not understand
much about Him but enough to claim Him as a friend.

Then the apostle John boldly and naively makes a strange
comment, "Teacher, we saw someone who does not follow us
casting out demons in Your name, and we forbade him because
he does not follow us" (verse 38). The attentive reader notices
the sharp contrast between the beginning of the narrative in
chapter 9 and John's comment. A day or so earlier, the disciples

of Jesus had not been able to cast out a demon from this little boy, yet they are Jesus' closest friends and disciples. And now, a disciple of Jesus states that he prevented someone else who did cast out demons in Jesus' name from doing so because this person is not in the inner group of Jesus' followers. The narrative begs the question: who is a true disciple of Jesus? One who follows Him and cannot cast out demons? Or one who does not follow Him but can cast out demons in His name?

Jesus answers: "Do not forbid him, for no one who works a miracle in My name can soon afterward speak evil of Me. For he who is not against us is on our side. For whoever gives you a cup of water to drink in My name, because you belong to Christ, assuredly, I say to you, he will by no means lose his reward" (verses 39, 40). What does this say of our discourse about other Christians? This story ought to challenge Seventh-day Adventists and all other Christians who claim to be followers of Jesus, the Messiah. It appears there is more to belonging than meets the eye.

In another narrative, in John 10, Jesus reveals He is the Good Shepherd and His sheep will know His voice. He then elaborates on the theme, "And other sheep I have which are not of this fold; them also I must bring, and they will hear My voice; and there will be one flock and one shepherd" (verse 16). The gathering movement of this metaphor is from the exterior to the interior. "They will hear My voice" and come in to form one flock. Jesus implies that during the years of His ministry, there were people who were His sheep, out there in the world, but who had not yet heard His voice. But when they would hear it, they would come and join Him. There would then be one flock with one shepherd. It is likely He may have had Pentecost in mind when He said this. Yet, when is this gathering to happen? Should Christians now seek to fulfill Christ's wish and seek to gather all of God's people in one fold? Or is it more plausible that this statement has eschatological implications, that at the second coming of Christ all of God's sheep will form one flock?

In any case, this statement challenges Seventh-day Adventists as they think about Christian unity. What does this say about my discourse concerning other Christians? God has His people in areas and in "flocks" that we know nothing of, and with the humility of Jesus we should be reaching out to other Christians and encouraging them in their spiritual journey, all the while, refraining from statements and actions that offend other Christians who claim to be followers of Jesus, yet do not live their relationship with Christ exactly as we do. These gospel stories invite us to generosity toward all who claim to be followers of Jesus.

Christ's high priestly prayer in John 17 is a reminder that He is still concerned about Christian unity today. His focus is not on organizational or structural unity, but on unity in faith, truth, and love. His prayer should be ours as we seek to solidify our faith in His sanctifying Word. Surely, love for one another should characterize our relationship with fellow Christians, however diverse our understanding of the gospel may be.

1. F. F. Bruce, *The Gospel of John* (Grand Rapids, MI: Eerdmans, 1983), 328.

2. Andreas J. Köstenberger, *John*, Baker Exegetical Commentary on the New Testament (Grand Rapids, MI: Baker Academic, 2004), 496.

3. Köstenberger, *John*, 497.

4. Peter J. Leithart, *The End of Protestantism: Pursuing Unity in a Fragmented Church* (Grand Rapids, MI: Brazos Press, 2016), 1 (emphasis in the original).

5. Gregg R. Allison, *Sojourners and Strangers: The Doctrine of the Church* (Wheaton, IL: Crossway, 2012), 170.

6. James Montgomery Boice, quoted in Richard D. Phillips, Philip G. Ryken, and Mark E. Dever, *The Church: One, Holy, Catholic, and Apostolic* (Phillipsburg, NJ: P & R Publishing, 2004), 28.

7. J. Marcellus Kik, *Ecumenism and the Evangelical* (Grand Rapids, MI: Baker Book House, 1958), 41–44.

8. Köstenberger, *John*, 498.

9. Ekkehardt Mueller, *The Letters of John* (Nampa, ID: Pacific Press®, 2009), 39.

10. Ellen G. White, *Testimonies for the Church* (Mountain View, CA: Pacific Press®, 1948), 4:17.

11. Peter C. Bouteneff, "The World Council of Churches: An Orthodox Perspective," in *Celebrating a Century of Ecumenism*, ed. John A. Radano (Grand Rapids, MI: Eerdmans, 2012), 15.

# CHAPTER 4

# Christ, the Key to Unity

The apostle Paul expressed a deep concern for unity among Christ's followers and made this the central theme of his epistle to the Ephesians. Ephesus was a major center of commerce and influence in Asia Minor at that time, and the Christian church in Ephesus included Jews, Gentiles, slaves, free people, and others from Europe and Asia Minor. Such a diverse group might have been as prone to conflict as the world in which they lived were it not for Jesus Christ and the unity they had in Him.

In this epistle, Paul's concept of unity has two dimensions: (1) unity in the church, where Jews and Gentiles are brought together in one Body—Christ, and (2) unity in the universe, in which all things in heaven and earth find their ultimate oneness in Christ. The source of this unity is Christ, His death, and His resurrection. More than thirty times in this epistle, Paul uses the expression "in Christ" or "with Christ" to show what God has accomplished for us and for the universe through the life, death, and resurrection of Jesus Christ. God's ultimate purpose in the plan of salvation is to reunify all things through Him. He is the key to unity, and four important unity themes emerge in the letter to the Ephesians.

### Blessings in Christ

Paul begins with a presentation of the blessings Christians have received in Christ. "Blessed be the God and Father of our Lord Jesus Christ, who has blessed us with every spiritual blessing in the heavenly places in Christ" (Ephesians 1:3). The followers of Jesus have much to praise God for because, through Jesus, He has adopted them to represent Him to the world. In Jesus, they have a bright future as ambassadors of the spiritual blessings they have received.

In this first passage, Paul uses various images to describe a new relationship with God, in Christ. Of these images, the image of adoption most closely addresses the theme of oneness and unity. In Christ, we have been adopted and now belong to the family of God. He "chose us in Him [Christ] before the foundation of the world, that we should be holy and without blame before Him in love, having predestined us to adoption as sons by Jesus Christ to Himself, according to the good pleasure of His will" (verses 4, 5).

The image of adoption refers to God's covenant with the children of Israel (see Deuteronomy 7:6–8). In the context of Paul's epistle, Gentiles who accept Jesus as the Messiah are also children of God, heirs of the promises made to Israel (Romans 8:17; Galatians 4:7). The benefit of this relationship with Christ is the foundation of all Christian unity.

This passage also tells us it has always been God's purpose to reunite all humanity in Christ. "Having made known to us the mystery of His will, according to His good pleasure which He purposed in Himself, that in the dispensation of the fullness of the times He might gather together in one all things in Christ, both which are in heaven and which are on earth—in Him" (Ephesians 1:9, 10). In God's family, knowing Jesus does not provide special status. We are all children of God, equally loved and cherished.

### Breaking down the wall

A second theme in the epistle is Paul's argument that the unity of the church is rooted in a new identity Christians receive in

Christ. As a result of sin and the events at the Tower of Babel, some of the deepest divisions among human beings are caused by differences in language, ethnicity, race, and religion. In many societies, different ethnic or religious groups dress distinctly. In other countries, identity cards indicate one's ethnicity or religion, creating a gateway for privileges and restrictions that people live with on a daily basis. When wars or conflicts arise, these distinctions often become catalysts for repression and violence against one another.

In Ephesians 2:11–18, Paul indicates a better way for the Christian community. He invites the Ephesians to remember what their lives were like before they received the grace of God in Christ. Cultural differences create animosity and conflict between people groups, but the good news is that in Christ we are all one people, with a common Savior and Lord. We all belong equally to the people of God. "But now in Christ Jesus you who were far off have been brought near by the blood of Christ" (verse 13).

According to Josephus, the ancient temple in Jerusalem had a wall of separation to distinguish the sections accessible only to ethnic Jews. This wall had an inscription on it that forbade any foreigners to go any farther, under pain of death.[1] It is this regulation that Paul was accused of transgressing when he entered the temple after his third missionary journey. He was arrested and charged with bringing into the Jewish section of the temple an Ephesian named Trophimus (Acts 21:29). This brings deeper meaning to Paul's argument that Christ "is our peace, who has made both [ethnic groups, Jews and Gentiles] one, and has broken down the middle wall of separation" (Ephesians 2:14). Whether this is a direct allusion to the Jerusalem temple partition wall or not, it remains a powerful image. "Modern readers, like those first readers in Ephesus, are probably best served by treating this as a straightforward image of separation."[2]

In Christ, all believers are spiritual descendants of Abraham and receive the circumcision of the heart. The physical circumcision that God required of Abraham pointed to the spiritual circumcision that all believers would receive in Christ (see

Deuteronomy 10:16). "In Him you were also circumcised with the circumcision made without hands, by putting off the body of the sins of the flesh, by the circumcision of Christ" (Colossians 2:11).

While the world experiences constant ethnic and religious conflicts, Paul argues that for all those who claim to be followers of Christ as Lord and Savior, Christ is "our peace." Such a spiritual relationship is the foundation of Christian unity—it is a spiritual unity that binds all Christians together. How unfortunate that for vast numbers of Christians who claim to be followers of Christ, the original human nature before knowing Christ (Ephesians 2:1–3) remains alive and hinders the fulfillment of this bond of unity. True unity in Christ must transform cultural differences to become reasons for celebration instead of cause for conflict. If all Christians, regardless of their church affiliations, realized and lived this new reality in Christ, churches would be renewed, communities and neighborhoods would be transformed, and the world would suffer much less war and conflict.

The new identity markers of Christ's followers are simple but crucial. To one another we are "no longer strangers and foreigners, but fellow citizens with the saints and members of the household of God" (Ephesians 2:19). Followers of Christ have a new identity that transcends all other ethnic, cultural, linguistic, and religious markers. As children of the same household and new citizens of God's kingdom, this new identity brings fresh challenges to the community of faith.

## One body

In the first verses of chapter 4, Paul expresses a third theme regarding his deep interest in the unity of the church. He begins with an exhortation to unity (verses 1–3) and follows with a list of the seven elements that unite believers (verses 4–6). Unity is simultaneously something that believers already possess, something that must be constantly worked on and maintained, and something that is the future goal toward which we strive (verse 13).

# Christ, the Key to Unity

Paul is practical in his advice to the Ephesians. This unity that exists between people of different cultural heritage and ethnic backgrounds is not a myth or a theoretical concept; it is a reality that requires them "to walk worthy of the calling with which you were called" (Ephesians 4:1). "Because of all that God has done for us in providing salvation and making us into a spiritual dwelling place of God in the spirit, a dwelling place in which Jew and Gentile are united as one, we should live like the people we have become."[3] Such followers of Christ exhibit lowliness, gentleness, longsuffering, and bearing with one another in love (verse 2). The practical outcome of these virtues and graces in the Christian's life helps "keep the unity of the Spirit in the bond of peace" (verse 3). All these attributes are rooted in love (1 Corinthians 13:1–7). The active practice of love preserves relationships among brothers and sisters and promotes peace and unity in the Christian community and beyond. Unity in the church manifests God's love in ways that people outside the church and the nations at large can observe in no other way. "It is important to realize that unity is something given by the Spirit, not something we create. It is based in the oneness of God and the oneness of the gospel, which works the same for all people."[4]

Verses 4 to 6 are often quoted in reference to church unity. "There is one body and one Spirit, just as you were called in one hope of your calling; one Lord, one faith, one baptism; one God and Father of all, who is above all, and through all, and in you all." The church unity Paul speaks of is theologically centered: on the Holy Spirit (one body, one Spirit, one hope), on Christ (one faith, one baptism, one Lord), and on the Father (one God and Father of all). According to Everett Ferguson, "These seven items are part of the 'givens' of Christianity. Unity is already provided by God in the most important things. Sharing these fundamental things gives a broad and strong basis for unity. In view of what unites, the things that divide seem less formidable. . . . In a sense, to be divided is to say God has not done enough to produce unity; it is to minimize the most important aspects of the Christian faith."[5]

During a period of time when Seventh-day Adventists witnessed large numerical growth and geographical expansion that challenged their unity, Ellen White offered the following insight on this chapter of the epistle to the Ephesians:

> The apostle exhorts his brethren to manifest in their lives the power of the truth which he had presented to them. By meekness and gentleness, forbearance and love, they were to exemplify the character of Christ and the blessings of His salvation. There is but one body, and one Spirit, one Lord, one faith. As members of the body of Christ all believers are animated by the same spirit and the same hope. Divisions in the church dishonor the religion of Christ before the world and give occasion to the enemies of truth to justify their course. Paul's instructions were not written alone for the church in his day. God designed that they should be sent down to us. What are we doing to preserve unity in the bonds of peace?[6]

### Church leaders and unity

A fourth theme on the unity of the church is God's provision for fostering the unity of the church through the spiritual gifts of leadership. In a sense, all Christians are ministers and servants of God and the gospel. At baptism every believer becomes involved in the mission of the church. Christ's commission in Matthew 28:19, 20 is given to all Christians: go, make disciples of all nations, baptize, and teach. The work of ministry is not given to a privileged few but to all who profess the name of Christ. Therefore, no one can claim exemption from service, and no church leader can claim a ministry exclusive to themselves. The spiritual gifts of leadership are given to benefit the unity of the church, and leaders are needed to foster, promote, and encourage unity. Jesus' style of leadership must guide the practice of ministry. He came to serve others and not to be served (Matthew 20:25–28).

Paul's list of gifts of leadership in Ephesians 4:11 ("some to be apostles, some prophets, some evangelists, and some pastors and teachers") tells us that these roles are for the express purpose of equipping God's people for the work of ministry (verse 12). It is the responsibility of specially gifted people within the church to help others fulfill their service for Christ and to edify the body of Christ "till we all come to the unity of the faith and of the knowledge of the Son of God, to a perfect man, to the measure of the stature of the fullness of Christ" (verse 13). The sixteenth-century French Reformer John Calvin, commenting on this concept, said, "Our true completeness and perfection consists in our being united into the Body of Christ."[7] God has always intended the church to be a community where His children are edified, strengthened, and perfected.

Yet, there is a strong tendency toward independence and a disdain for accountability. Western society, in particular, is plagued with this inclination. Paul reminds us, however, that no Christian is alone in this world and that we form a community of faith with spiritual leaders to help and encourage one another in our common journey. Together, we are part of the body of Christ in which we find strength and encouragement. In the same manner, the epistle to the Hebrews exhorts, "Let us hold fast the confession of our hope without wavering, for He who promised is faithful. And let us consider one another in order to stir up love and good works, not forsaking the assembling of ourselves together, as is the manner of some, but exhorting one another, and so much the more as you see the Day approaching" (Hebrews 10:23–25).

A dynamic community where unity exists and is encouraged is also characterized by fellowship and service. Seventh-day Adventists often comment that wherever they go they find brothers and sisters in Christ. Such brotherhood is a fruit of the Spirit. Gregg Allison observes that "the fellowship and connectedness that are sensed by believers crossing into different cultures and meeting Christians from different nationalities, ethnicities, linguistic groups, socioeconomic status, political systems, educational levels, and religious backgrounds, point toward another factor enhancing unity: membership in the universal body of Christ."[8]

One in Christ

1. Josephus, *Antiquities of the Jews* 15.11.5 and *The Wars of the Jews* 5.5.2.

2. Stephen E. Fowl, *Ephesians: A Commentary*, The New Testament Library (Louisville, KY: Westminster John Knox Press, 2012), 91.

3. Max Anders, *Galatians, Ephesians, Philippians & Colossians*, The Holman New Testament Commentary (Nashville, TN: Broadman & Holman, 1999), 148.

4. Klyne Snodgrass, *Ephesians*, The NIV Application Commentary (Grand Rapids, MI: Zondervan, 1996), 198.

5. Quoted in Gregg R. Allison, *Sojourners and Strangers: The Doctrine of the Church* (Wheaton, IL: Crossway, 2012), 172, 173.

6. Ellen G. White, *Testimonies for the Church* (Mountain View, CA: Pacific Press®, 1948), 5:239.

7. John Calvin, *The Epistles of Paul the Apostle to the Galatians, Ephesians, Philippians and Colossians*, trans. T. H. L. Parker (Grand Rapids, MI: Eerdmans, 1965), 181.

8. Allison, *Sojourners and Strangers*, 173.

# Early Experiences of Church Unity

The experience of the early Christian church teaches that unity is the result of a shared spiritual experience. In the first chapters of the book of Acts, we see that solid bonds of fellowship are forged in a common spiritual journey and experience. The experience of Jesus' disciples after His ascension to heaven is testimony to the power of Bible study, prayer, and fellowship in creating unity and harmony among believers of various backgrounds.

Their common spiritual bond also affected how they related to one another's physical needs. Certainly the same experience, or one similar, is still possible among God's people today. Robert Rayburn comments that "fellowship is a particularly important element in corporate worship. . . . There is no substitute to the Christian for the realization of the spiritual bond which unites him with other believers and with the Lord Jesus Christ. . . . Jesus Christ first brings a soul to Himself, but then He always unites that soul to other believers in His body, the church."[1]

## Days of preparation

In the last hours He spent with His disciples before His death, Jesus promised that He would not leave them alone. Another Comforter, the Holy Spirit, would be sent to accompany them in their ministry. The Spirit would help them remember many things Jesus had said and done (John 14:26) and would guide them in discovering more truths (John 16:13). On the day of His ascension, Jesus renewed this promise. "You shall be baptized with the Holy Spirit not many days from now. . . . You shall receive power when the Holy Spirit has come upon you" (Acts 1:5, 8). The Holy Spirit's power would enable the disciples to be Jesus' witnesses in Jerusalem, Judea, Samaria, and to the end of the earth (verse 8). The reception of the Holy Spirit was for one purpose: to tell the story of Jesus to those who had not heard it.

Thus, while the 120 disciples waited for the fulfillment of this promise, they "continued with one accord in prayer and supplication" (verse 14). These ten days between the ascension of Jesus and Pentecost were probably a period of intense spiritual preparation, a kind of spiritual retreat during which the disciples shared their memories of Jesus: His actions, His teachings, and His miracles. They recounted what He meant to them and sought to understand the meaning of His death and resurrection. They were of "one accord in prayer and supplication," demonstrating that the best preparation for effective witnessing is to wait in prayer.

Arthur Patzia comments,

> When Luke describes the early Christian community in Jerusalem, he indicates that prayer was an important expression of their faith (Acts 2:42, 46; 3:1). This is not surprising given the significance of personal and corporate prayer in Judaism, as described in the Old Testament and practiced in temple and synagogue worship. Those who followed Jesus as disciples during his earthly ministry not only observed the importance of prayer in his personal life but were taught how they themselves were to pray (Mt 6:9-13; Lk 11:2-4).
>
> Hence, it is quite natural that his followers who met in the upper room after the ascension "were constantly devoting themselves to prayer" (Acts 1:14).[2]

# Early Experiences of Church Unity

Elsewhere in the book of Acts, Luke gives numerous references to the role of prayer in the early Christian community. He refers to the prayers of Stephen (Acts 7:59), Saul (Acts 9:11), Peter (Acts 10:9; 11:15), Cornelius (Acts 10:30, 31), and Paul and Silas (Acts 16:25). Luke also mentions moments when groups of Christians prayed together: selecting Matthias to replace Judas (Acts 1:24), praying for Peter's release from prison (Acts 12:5, 12), and commissioning Barnabas and Paul (Acts 13:3). Additionally, in many of Paul's letters he mentions his constant prayers for each church (Romans 1:9; Philippians 1:4, 9; Colossians 1:3, 9; 1 Thessalonians 1:2; 2 Thessalonians 1:11). He also encouraged people to pray for him and their communities (Romans 8:26; 12:12; Philippians 4:6; Colossians 4:2).[3] It is obvious that prayer was central in the daily worship and ministry of the early church.

## Undoing the Tower of Babel

At the close of the ten days of spiritual preparation, Pentecost came to a dramatic climax. Acts 2:1 says that just before the Holy Spirit was poured upon the disciples, they were all together, of "one accord in one place." In the Old Testament, Pentecost was the second of three major feasts every male Israelite was obligated to attend. It was held fifty days (in Greek, *pentekoste*, "fiftieth") after Passover. During this feast, Hebrews presented to God the firstfruits of their summer harvest as an offering of thanksgiving.

The Feast of Pentecost fell during May to mid-June, when traveling conditions were easier for distant Jews journeying to Jerusalem. Pentecost was also a joyous feast, perhaps explaining the reference to too much drinking (Acts 2:13). But the miracle of Pentecost was each listener hearing the gospel message in his own language (verses 6–8). More than any other moment, this phenomenon "underscores the divine initiative in making possible the mission God has commissioned. In a real sense, God is bringing the message of the gospel home to those who hear it."[4] Jews from all over the Roman Empire who have come to Jerusalem for this feast hear the message of Jesus, the Messiah, in their own languages. From Jerusalem the story rushes to the ends of the world. This is also the beginning of the breaking down of ethnic and racial barriers that will become more prominent later in the book of Acts.

In an extraordinary way, Pentecost undoes the dispersion of the original human family and the formation of linguistic groups at the Tower of Babel (Genesis 11:5–9). It marked the inauguration of the Christian church, a reunification of the people of God under the new reality that Jesus is the Messiah, the Savior of the world. What was lost at Babel is brought back, in part, at Pentecost. It is a spiritual unification, not a physical one. Diversity of languages continues after Pentecost, but the gospel message is symbolically proclaimed to people from the entire known world. They will then return to their homelands, sharing what they have learned and experienced. It is this gospel message that reunites the human family.

The Holy Spirit empowers Christian witnesses to carry the gospel to the entire world, "to create a worldwide people of God, united by a common confession in the lordship of Christ."[5] Pentecost marks the beginning of the Christian church, empowered by the Holy Spirit for its mission. Just as Pentecost celebrates the firstfruits of the summer harvest, it becomes a symbol for the beginning of the gospel's spiritual harvest, in Jerusalem and beyond.

### Unity of fellowship

In response to Peter's sermon and appeal for repentance and salvation, three thousand people decided to accept Jesus as the Messiah, the fulfillment of the Old Testament promises to Israel. Luke then describes the first activities of these early followers of Jesus: "And they continued steadfastly in the apostles' doctrine and fellowship, in the breaking of bread, and in prayers" (Acts 2:42). This fledgling community of new believers engaged first in learning from the apostles the teachings of Jesus. They likely heard about His life and ministry, His teachings, parables, and sermons, and His miracles. They reminisced about Jesus' last days, His trial, crucifixion, and resurrection, and His promise to come again.

Luke states that they also spent time breaking bread and praying. It is unclear whether the breaking of bread is a direct allusion to the Lord's Supper or simply a reference to sharing meals together, as verse 46 seems to imply. The mention of fellowship certainly infers that this new community spent time together, often and regularly, both in the Jerusalem temple, which still served as the center of their devotions and worship, and in their private homes. They shared an intimate life, eating together and praying together. It was all intentional and purposeful. Prayer was clearly a vital element in this community of faith, an essential part of spiritual growth. These close relationships led them to meaningful time spent in worship as they "steadfastly" pursued learning the message of Jesus.

It is also interesting to note that the result of this steadfast fellowship generated good relationships in Jerusalem—the new believers are described as "having favor with all the people" (verse 47). The character of their faith and fellowship was positively noticed by people around them, and "this attitude of daily worship in all things and love for one another overflowed into evangelism as a part of everyday life."[6]

## Generosity and greed

The book of Acts tells us that one of the natural outgrowths of the fellowship experienced by Jesus' followers soon after Pentecost was their mutual support of each other. "Now all who believed were together, and had all things in common, and sold their possessions and goods, and divided them among all, as anyone had need" (Acts 2:44, 45). This sharing of common goods is not a requirement of the community. Rather, it is a voluntary outgrowth of their love for one another in the fellowship they experience and is a concrete expression of their spiritual unity. This mutual support continued for some time, and we are given more details about it in chapters 4 and 5. It is also a theme we find in other places in the New Testament (1 Corinthians 16:1, 2; 2 Corinthians 8:1–6; Acts 11:27–30).

One of Jesus' apocalyptic parables sets the stage to understand the generosity of the new community of believers. In the parable of the sheep and the goats (Matthew 25:31–46), Jesus taught that on the day of judgment His followers would be identified by their treatment of the less fortunate and the marginalized among them.

> "Then the King will say to those on His right hand, 'Come, you blessed of My Father, inherit the kingdom prepared for you from the foundation of the world: for I was hungry and you gave Me food; I was thirsty and you gave Me drink; I was a stranger and you took Me in; I was naked and you clothed Me; I was sick and you visited Me; I was in prison and you came to Me.' Then the righteous will answer Him, saying, 'Lord, when did we see You hungry and feed You, or thirsty and give You drink? When did we see You a stranger and take You in, or naked and clothe You? Or when did we see You sick, or in prison, and come to You?' And the King will answer and say to them, 'Assuredly, I say to you, inasmuch as you did it to one of the least of these My brethren, you did it to Me' " (Matthew 25:34–40).

This parable is not teaching salvation by social works, but it articulates the need for the followers of Jesus to live by the same ethical and social values that characterized the ministry of Jesus. The apostle James also required the same of his readers (James 2:14–26). These demands were not new or strange to the people of the Old Testament. The books of Moses and some of the prophets also emphasized such social and ethical "good works" as evidences of covenantal faithfulness to God (Exodus 22:21; Deuteronomy 15:7, 11; Isaiah 58:6, 7; Ezekiel 18:7, 16; Proverbs 14:31). It appears this same ethical and social faithfulness to the less fortunate characterized the early Christian community and magnified its common expression of unity.

It is in this context that Acts 4 and 5 describe how the early church in Jerusalem shared everything in common. Barnabas is introduced for the first time and appears to be a wealthy person who owned land. He sells his property for the benefit of the community and brings the money to the apostles (Acts 4:36, 37). In this story, Barnabas serves as a positive example of the early church's spirit of fellowship and generosity. But in contrast to Barnabas are the examples of Ananias and Sapphira (Acts 5:1–11). There is perhaps no greater way to destroy fellowship and brotherly love than with the sin of selfishness and greed—seeking one's own private interest over those of the community. Though unsavory, Luke honestly shares this story about less virtuous people in the community. Today, many local church communities are still affected by the sin of greed that some hold on to, bringing much harm to fellowship and unity.

In the Ten Commandments (Exodus 20:1–17), the last commandment about covetousness is unlike the others. While other commandments speak of actions that visibly transgress God's will for humanity, the last commandment is about what is hidden in the heart. The sin of covetousness is not an action; rather, it is a thought process. Covetousness, and its companion selfishness, are not visible sins. They are a state of human nature, becoming visible only when manifested in selfish actions. In a sense, the last commandment is the root of all the evil actions condemned by the other commandments. In the lives of Ananias and Sapphira, covetousness, greed, and self-serving are desires attributed to Satan. Of course, this is no excuse for their wrong actions, but it is clear that cosmic forces are at play in this situation. God is lied to as Satan seeks to infiltrate the early church.

The sharing of one's resources is seen as a visible expression of unity in the early church. The generosity described in the early chapters of Acts continues with Paul inviting the churches he has established in Macedonia and Achaia to make a contribution for the poor in Jerusalem (Acts 11:27–30; Galatians 2:10; Romans 15:26; 1 Corinthians 16:1–4; 2 Corinthians 8:1–7). That gift becomes a tangible expression that churches, consisting mainly of Gentile believers, care and love their brothers and sisters of Jewish heritage in Jerusalem. In spite of cultural differences, they form one body of Christ and together cherish the same gospel of salvation. For Paul, too, new covenant faithfulness in the early church is manifested by how Christian believers care for the less fortunate among them.

Soon after Pentecost, the early church gives a few examples of how they experienced unity. As the Holy Spirit formed this new community from a diverse group of ethnic people, they experienced rapid growth because Jesus' disciples had first intentionally prepared themselves for the outpouring of the promised Holy Spirit. After Pentecost, the Holy Spirit continued to transform this new community as it lived in fellowship, learning from the apostles the message of the gospel of Jesus Christ, eating together, and praying together. Unity, however, did not happen without intentional commitment on the part of all believers. The leaders of the early community saw it as their ministry to foster unity. Their unity also manifested itself in their generosity toward each other.

Although today's social customs are considerably different from those of the early church, we can still learn from their experience. The unity we have in Christ is both encouraged and made visible in a number of ways. Our unity in Christ today will benefit from our intentional spiritual preparation for the reception of the Holy Spirit, from regular fellowship, the breaking of bread, prayer, and a common response of caring for the less fortunate.

---

1. Robert G. Rayburn, *O Come, Let Us Worship* (Grand Rapids, MI: Baker Book House, 1980), 91.

2. Arthur G. Patzia, *The Emergence of the Church: Context, Growth, Leadership & Worship* (Downers Grove, IL: InterVarsity, 2001), 205, 206.

3. Patzia, *The Emergence of the Church*, 206.

4. Darrell L. Bock, *Acts*, Baker Exegetical Commentary on the New Testament (Grand Rapids, MI: Baker Academic, 2007), 102.

5. John B. Polhill, *Acts*, The New American Commentary (Nashville, TN: Broadman Press, 1992), 106.

6. John-Michael Wong, *Opening Up Acts* (Leominster, UK: Day One Publications, 2010), 31.

CHAPTER

# Images of Unity

The Bible uses images and metaphors to describe the church, its activities, and its basic identity. In 1960, New Testament scholar Paul S. Minear published the book *Images of the Church in the New Testament*, in which he catalogued 96 metaphors of the church.[1] Among these metaphors and images, he highlighted four: "the people of God," "the new creation," "the fellowship of faith," and "the body of Christ." Other theologians have focused on three primary metaphors. They come from a Trinitarian perspective and are identified as "the people of God," "body of Christ," and "the fellowship of the Spirit." Like all metaphors these images are not complete by themselves, but together as a whole, they help us visualize God's relationship to the church and our relationship with the church. They clarify important aspects of unity and the relationship of each member to the community of faith.

## The people of God

Writing to believers in Asia Minor, the apostle Peter described God's "own special people" as "a chosen generation, a royal priesthood, a holy nation" (1 Peter 2:9). These expressions indicate that God's people are established for a special purpose: to "proclaim the praises of Him who called you out of darkness into His marvelous light." They also echo a key passage from the book of Exodus. Just before He proclaimed the Ten Commandments on Mount Sinai, God established His covenant with the people of Israel. "Now therefore, if you will indeed obey My voice and keep My covenant, then you shall be a special treasure to Me above all people; for all the earth is Mine. And you shall be to Me a kingdom of priests and a holy nation" (Exodus 19:5, 6). Elsewhere in the Old Testament we find similar descriptions of God's people:

- chosen generation (Deuteronomy 10:15; Isaiah 43:20, 21)
- royal priesthood (Isaiah 61:6)
- holy nation (Deuteronomy 7:6)

In Peter's mind, there was obvious continuity between God's people of the old covenant and believers in Jesus, the Messiah of the new covenant. This image emphasizes that the church is about people, and not just any people—but the people of God, the people who belong to God, the redeemed people who claim God as their Father and Savior. The metaphor also underscores the concept that God's people on earth have never been without a plan of salvation.

Beginning with Adam, continuing with the patriarchs, and culminating with Abraham, God has covenanted with His people to be representatives of His love, mercy, and justice to the world. The purpose for God's people has always been the same: to praise God and reflect His character (1 Peter 2:9; Isaiah 9:2). "God acquired the church as His own special possession in order that its members might reflect His precious traits of character in their own lives and proclaim His goodness and mercy to all men."[2]

When Moses and Peter qualify God's people as a "holy people" (Deuteronomy 7:6; 1 Peter 2:9), they beg the question, what group of people or nation today deserves the label of "holy nation"? The resounding answer is simple: none. All nations or ethnic groups are composed of sinners who do not deserve the love of God. But Scripture teaches that the selection and establishment of God's people was based entirely on His love, not the merits of human beings in any age. The formation of God's people is an act of loving creation, and in spite of sin and apostasy, God kept His promise to Abraham to save His people. The election of God's people was an act of His grace, just like their salvation. This theme is a strong reminder of our common roots in the unmerited grace of God. As people of God, we are all united in His grace.

One further implication of this metaphor is parity. Parity among the people of God. German theologian Hans Küng rightly notes, "If we see the Church as the people of God, it is clear that the Church can never be merely a particular class or caste, a group of officials or a clique within the fellowship of the faithful. The Church is always and in all cases the *whole* people of God, the *whole* ecclesia, the *whole* fellowship of the faithful. Everyone belongs to the chosen race, the royal priesthood, the holy nation. . . . All members of the Church are equal in this."[3]

### The household of God

A few verses earlier, in the same chapter in which he refers to God's people, Peter also described Christians as "living stones" (1 Peter 2:5) and used the metaphor of a house or building. Paul, in Ephesians, uses the same image. "Now, therefore, you are no longer strangers and foreigners, but fellow citizens with the saints and members of the household of God, having been built on the foundation of the apostles and prophets, Jesus Christ Himself being the chief cornerstone, in whom the whole building, being fitted together, grows into a holy temple in the Lord, in whom you also are being built together for a dwelling place of God in the Spirit" (Ephesians 2:19–22; see also 1 Timothy 3:15). Two images of the church are connected together in this passage: one inert, a house or building; the other alive, a household of people. The first is a metaphor of physical structures that highlight the intricate and interdependent nature of human relationships in the church. The second is about the relationships of people who live in the house of God.

The metaphor of the house certainly evokes a sense of permanency and strength. A stone is not very valuable by itself, but when bonded with other stones, it becomes a structure that can withstand the storms of life. No Christian can be a stone alone but must be associated with others to form the house of God. For an edifice to be solid, it must rest on a strong foundation, and for both Peter and Paul, Jesus Christ is this foundation, the "cornerstone" of the house of God (1 Peter 2:5–8; 1 Corinthians 3:11). The church would cease to exist if it did not make Christ the very foundation of its life and activities because the church is all about Jesus Christ, His message, His death and resurrection, and His soon return. The church forms a community of believers, united in their mission to share good news about Jesus to the world. The activities of the church must reflect this reality, and the church's mission must be more than a loose collection of ideas and projects. The church has no other reason to exist, except to give glory to God for salvation in Jesus and the privilege of sharing this message with the world.

The second image of a household is also meaningful. This one rests on the relationships people have between themselves. The Seventh-day Adventist statement of fundamental belief on the church (no. 12) states, "The church is God's family; adopted by Him as children, its members live on the basis of the new covenant."[4] It is a familiar image of father and mother, brothers and sisters, and the extended family members. Ties between family members can be strong, and the accompanying loyalties often transcend all ties with other people. This metaphor underscores that all believers are part of one big family. Not only are we tied together because we belong to the human family through our common ancestor Adam, but we are also related to Jesus, the Second Adam, through our common new-birth experience (Acts 17:26; 2 Corinthians 5:17).

In response to Peter's comment about the disciples' sacrifice to follow Him, Jesus said, "Assuredly, I say to you, there is no one who has left house or brothers or sisters or father or mother or wife or children or lands, for My sake and the gospel's, who shall not receive a hundredfold now in this time—houses and brothers and sisters and mothers and children and lands, with persecutions—and in the age to come, eternal life" (Mark 10:29, 30). The family of God, the Christian community, alleviates the disruptions created by sacrifices made for the sake of the gospel. Jesus' promise that His disciples would one day become a large family in His Father's house must have given them great courage (John 14:2, 3).

### The temple of the Holy Spirit

Another building imagery Paul uses is that of the temple of God or of the Holy Spirit. It is the metaphor of a costly and valuable building and refers to the most holy and precious edifice of the ancient Near East. "Do you not know that you are the temple of God and that the Spirit of God dwells in you? If anyone defiles the temple of God, God will destroy him. For the temple of God is holy, which temple you are" (1 Corinthians 3:16, 17).

The presence of the Holy Spirit among God's people is an important teaching of the New Testament. Jesus predicted that after His departure, He would send a Comforter to continue to guide His disciples into all truth (John 14:16, 26; 15:26; 16:13). In the book of Acts, the Holy Spirit guides the witness of the early church, and the growth of the Christian community is the direct result of the presence of the Spirit (Acts 4:31; 5:32; 9:31). Even the establishment of the first Christian communities in Greece was the result of the Holy Spirit's guidance in Paul's ministry (Acts 16:6–10), and Paul believed that the Holy Spirit had formed the Corinthian community (1 Corinthians 2:1–16). In fact, from the Day of Pentecost, the church is the creation of the Holy Spirit.

In the first letter to the Corinthians, Paul refers to what he considers to be challenges to unity: "For . . . there are envy, strife, and divisions among you" (1 Corinthians 3:3). These attitudes and behaviors are real threats to Christian unity and cause God's presence to withdraw from His temple. In other words, conflict in the church destroys God's temple. So when Paul sensed that numerous divisions and strange teachings were threatening the life of the community, he became defensive and appealed to their spiritual understanding.

In 1 Corinthians 3:16, 17, Paul is obviously not referring to a physical temple or place of residence for God. Early Christians did not own temples or churches as Christians do today. The Greek of the New Testament makes a distinction between a "you" singular to refer to one person and a "you" plural to refer to many people. Here, it is the latter, and Paul is speaking to the entire Christian community in Corinth. The metaphor refers to a corporate image: together, the Christians in Corinth form the temple of the Holy Spirit, and in a spiritual sense, God resides among them. In the ancient Near East, the temple was the physical dwelling place for the gods. For Paul, God resides within the Christian fellowship, hence his warning that anyone who attempts to destroy this fellowship will suffer the consequences of the judgment. The unity of believers is at the core of this fellowship and the blessing of God's presence.

### The body of Christ

Possibly the best-known image of the church and one that speaks best about the unity of its varied parts is the body of Christ. This metaphor is also found in the writings of the apostle Paul. "For as the body is one and has many members, but all the members of that one body, being many, are one body, so also is Christ. . . . Now you are the body of Christ, and members individually" (1 Corinthians 12:12, 27). Just as the body is a unit, comprised of different parts with unique functions and responsibilities, so the church is the body of Christ.

This image speaks directly to us as a church. In the last few decades, the Seventh-day Adventist Church has grown by leaps and bounds, and our diversity is extensive. Ethnic, racial, cultural, educational, age, and gender differences must not be permitted to divide us in Christ. On the contrary, they must enhance unity. At the foot of the cross we are equal, brothers and sisters in Christ. As the world around us becomes more and more fragmented, the church must demonstrate that unity in diversity is attainable. God's people are called to demonstrate the healing and reconciling power of the gospel, that all nations can be one in Christ.

Paul's teaching in 1 Corinthians 12 conveys the profound reality that authentic Christian unity is not just *in* diversity, and certainly not *in spite of* diversity, but rather *through* diversity. We should not be surprised that the Holy Spirit is the source of these expressions of diversity. Just as the human body is incredibly unified and amazingly diverse, so it is with the body of Christ. From this perspective, it is not wise to rank diversity in an effort to weight some aspects of it as more essential than others. They are all needed to express the completeness and richness of the body of Christ. In fact, for Paul, there is no unity without diversity.

Through the blood of Christ, God's purpose was to reconcile humanity in one body (Ephesians 2:13–16) where human distinctions are blended in Christ. Amazingly, Paul tells us how this ideal can be accomplished. "Christ is the head of the church; and He is the Savior of the body" (Ephesians 5:23). "And He is the head of the body, the church" (Colossians 1:18). As each believer is spiritually connected to Christ in baptism (Romans 6:1–6), the entire body is therefore nourished with the same spiritual food.

Lutheran theologian Wolfhart Pannenberg comments, "Calling the church the body of Christ is no mere metaphor nor is it just one of the biblical ways of depicting the nature of the church. Instead, the realism of the inseparable union of believers with Christ that finds expression in the idea of the church as the body of Christ is basic to an understanding of the church as a fellowship of believers and hence also as the people of God. The church is a fellowship of believers only on the basis of the participation of each individual in the one Lord."[5] As we have already discovered, our common relationship in the Lord is visible as we live out this union in the study of the Word of God, fervent prayer, and shared worship.

## Sheep and Shepherd

In the modern world's large cities, it is rare to see animal husbandry of any kind. Most people know little of the relationship between sheep and shepherds. However, when Jesus told this parable, people understood him well. When He declared, "I am the good shepherd" (John 10:11), they immediately recognized the allusion to Psalm 23:1, "The LORD is my shepherd." The image was not only clear; it was also full of emotional value that made it vivid. In ancient Near Eastern culture, and still today in the Middle East, a shepherd is known as a faithful, patient, and tenacious person. Regardless of the difficulties encountered, a shepherd will care for the sheep. The figure of a shepherd, illustrating the character of God and His relationship to His people, is one of Scripture's dearest images.

Describing God's people as sheep is also an interesting image. An impression we often have of sheep is their harmless and defenseless nature, making them reliant on a good shepherd for protection and guidance. Sometimes, sheep will inadvertently get lost, and the shepherd will track them down and bring them back to the fold (Luke 15:3–7). Lambs often need to be carried, requiring extra care. Patience and understanding is needed to care for sheep. In many ways, this image perfectly represents the church. The Christian believer has nothing to fear and everything to gain in a relationship with the divine Shepherd.

Jesus also emphasized in this parable the importance of listening to the shepherd's voice. When conditions require it, it is possible to protect a few flocks of sheep by placing them in the same enclosure or sheepfold. How can they be separated later? All that is required is for the shepherd to stand at the door of the enclosure and call. His sheep will recognize his voice and come to him. "And when he brings out his own sheep, he goes before them; and the sheep follow him, for they know his voice" (John 10:4). Listening to the voice of the Shepherd is crucial for the church. The ultimate unity and safety of God's people depend on their proximity to Him.

This survey of church metaphors teaches the nuances of

unity in Jesus. The New Testament employs metaphors to illustrate both the nature and mission of the church. More important, these metaphors teach that God is attentively watching over and protecting His people. Finally, these images teach that God's people are intricately linked with each other. The Father, Son, and Holy Spirit shape the unity of Christian believers into one family. Together, they form the people of God, the body of Christ, and the temple of the Holy Spirit.

———

1. Paul S. Minear, *Images of the Church in the New Testament* (Louisville, KY: Westminster John Knox, 1960, 2004). See also John K. McVay, "Biblical Metaphors for the Church and Adventist Ecclesiology," *Andrews University Seminary Studies* 44, no. 2 (2006): 285–315.

2. Francis D. Nichol, ed., *Seventh-day Adventist Bible Commentary*, vol. 7 (Washington, DC: Review and Herald®, 1980), 562.

3. Hans Küng, *The Church*, trans. Ray and Rosaleen Ockenden (New York: Sheed and Ward, 1967), 125 (emphasis in the original).

4. "Our Beliefs: The Church," Adventist.org, https://www.adventist.org/en /beliefs/church/the-church/.

5. Wolfhart Pannenberg, *Systematic Theology*, trans. Geoffrey W. Bromiley, (Grand Rapids, MI: Eerdmans, 1998), 3:102.

7

# When Conflicts Arise

A difficult task for any Christian community is to maintain unity when grappling with differences of opinion on matters of identity and mission. Often, conflict in such matters cannot be brushed aside without devastating consequences. In this regard, today's Christian communities are no different from those of the New Testament. Early Christians also faced clashes arising from perceived interpersonal prejudices and from serious differences over interpretation of key Old Testament stories and practices. These conflicts could have destroyed the church in its infancy had it not been for thoughtful apostles and leaders who sought resolution through the study of Scripture and the guidance of the Holy Spirit. While it is true the early church experienced tremendous unity, over time it also faced inner conflict that jeopardized this unity and threatened its survival.

### Ethnic prejudices and favoritism
Acts 6 tells the story of the apostles selecting seven men to help them in their ministry. This process is framed in the context of a serious conflict within the fledgling community of believers. Though unintentional, the apostles appeared to favor widows of Hebrew heritage over widows of Greek heritage, providing the latter with less food than their Hebrew counterparts.[1]

However, whether intended or not, this favoritism toward one ethnic group was misplaced and caused some believers to wonder about equity and fairness in their community. Jesus had shown no favoritism toward others (Luke 20:21), and it appeared as if the apostles had forgotten this. This conflict threatened church unity because church leaders, appointed by Jesus, were perceived as ineffective and biased in their ministry. This was indeed a serious accusation. "No man, or even one set of men, could continue to bear these burdens alone," comments Ellen White, "without imperiling the future prosperity of the church. There was necessity for a further distribution of the responsibilities which had been borne so faithfully by a few during the earlier days of the church."[2]

The simple steps taken by the early church to solve this misunderstanding are valuable. First, the apostles listened carefully to the complaints of Greek-speaking believers and asked them for a solution. They relied on the group with the complaint to select seven men to become their associates, and these seven, all from Greek-speaking heritage, were men "of good reputation, full of the Holy Spirit and wisdom" (Acts 6:3). The ministry of the apostles, which up to then had been to both preach the word of God and distribute food to widows, was divided into two groups, each performing an equally valuable ministry for the proclamation of the gospel. Luke uses the same word (*diakonia*) to refer to both the ministry of the apostles to preach the word of God (verse 4) and to the ministry of the distribution of food (verse 1). The appointment of seven men, traditionally called deacons (although the New Testament does not call them as such), relieved the tension in the church at Jerusalem.

One can marvel at how such a simple solution averted a major conflict in the early church. Even a church led by Jesus' apostles could experience conflicts, and the story proves that no church is perfect. This solution teaches important lessons for today's church. In this case, the apostles trusted the group with the complaint to make the right choice and to offer the right solution. This is an amazing insight into interpersonal conflict and shows how resolution can be reached when each party believes the other is equally led by the Holy Spirit.[3]

### The conversion of Gentiles

The conversion of Gentiles to the gospel of Jesus is an event in the book of Acts that sets the stage for the greatest conflict in the life of the early church, one that would threaten its very existence and mission. Yet, surprisingly, the problem originated with two God-given dreams.

In Acts 10:9–16, the apostle Peter receives a bizarre dream while waiting for his meal. In the dream he saw a lowered sheet filled with animals, reptiles, and birds. As he gazed at the curious spectacle a voice from heaven said, "Rise, Peter; kill and eat" (verse 13). He is shocked by the vision because as a faithful Jew he had never partaken of unclean or defiled foods, as the Law requires (see Leviticus 11; Ezekiel 4:14; Daniel 1:8). But the intent of this dream was not about what to eat or not eat. It's important to remember that in the first decades of Christianity, the Jesus movement was primarily a Jewish subgroup made up of Jews who had accepted Jesus as the promised Messiah. These early Christians were faithful Jews and obeyed the Law as they had been taught. They did not consider the gospel of Jesus Christ as having erased or abolished the Old Testament prescriptions about what food to eat or avoid (see Matthew 5:17–20).

Strangely, a couple days earlier, a Roman centurion named Cornelius, living in Caesarea Maritima, on the coast of the Mediterranean Sea, had also received a dream. This man was "a devout man and one who feared God with all his household, who gave alms generously to the people, and prayed to God always" (Acts 10:2). In a vision, an angel appeared to him and gave him clear directions to send someone to Joppa to find a disciple of Jesus by the name of Simon (verses 4–6). It is obvious the Holy Spirit was guiding this set of circumstances to lead the early church in an unexpected direction, a direction God had predicted many years before.

Although Gentiles had previously been converted to Judaism and had become followers of Jesus (for example, Nicolas in

Acts 6:5), this is the first time a Gentile is accepting the gospel. This event highlighted a contentious issue that the early church had to face: circumcision. Early Christians were all Jews and believed that for a man to be part of God's covenant people, he had to be circumcised. The instructions in the Bible about this requirement were clear and unmistakable (Genesis 17:10; Acts 15:5). Since Jesus had not come to abolish the Law and the Prophets (Matthew 5:17), early believers in Jesus did not think this requirement had changed.

Yet, the Holy Spirit was preparing the way for God's plan to receive Gentiles into the fellowship of the Christian community without first being circumcised and becoming Jews. This development would fulfill Old Testament prophecies that predicted the Gentiles' positive response to God's invitation (Amos 9:11, 12; Isaiah 43:9; 56:6). Although Peter and his friends were at first hesitant to visit with Cornelius and share the gospel, what convinced Peter that this was indeed God's will was the outpouring of the Holy Spirit on Cornelius and his household. The outpouring was similar to what the disciples of Jesus had experienced on the Day of Pentecost (Acts 10:44–47).

If the Holy Spirit could be given to Gentiles in the same way as it was given to Jews, then it was evident that being circumcised was not prerequisite to becoming a believer in Jesus, the Messiah. The new covenant was therefore founded on faith in Jesus and not on physical circumcision. This conclusion set the stage for major theological and cultural conflict among early Christians. Should circumcision be required of Gentiles converting to the gospel? The Holy Spirit was leading in this matter, and Peter rightly understood from his vision and his experience with Cornelius that God shows no partiality or favoritism regarding the good news about Jesus (Acts 10:34).

### The Spirit is leading
Reports of what happened in Caesarea soon reached the leaders of the Christian community in Jerusalem, and they asked Peter to give an account of the events. They were offended by Peter's

behavior because according to their understanding of the Law of Moses, faithful Jews were not allowed to eat with Gentiles (Acts 11:3). Questions were raised about the legitimacy of Peter's actions and his decision to baptize these Gentiles (without the prior requirement of circumcision), and Peter carefully explained the events. There were witnesses (verse 12) to certify that the Holy Spirit had indeed manifested His presence in the same way it had at Pentecost. The guidance and leading of the Holy Spirit in this case was unassailable, and the supernatural gift was acknowledged. "When they heard these things they became silent; and they glorified God, saying, 'Then God has also granted to the Gentiles repentance to life' " (verse 18).

Perhaps leaders in Jerusalem thought that the story of Cornelius and his household would be an exception and that such an experience would not be repeated. However, the Holy Spirit thought otherwise. As persecution after Stephen's death (Acts 8:1) scattered the disciples of Jesus beyond Jerusalem and Judea, they began preaching in Samaria, Phoenicia, Cyprus, and Antioch. More and more Gentiles accepted Jesus as their Savior, just as He had predicted (Acts 1:8).

"Not all the problems were solved, however," notes John Polhill.

> Not all the Jewish Christians were satisfied with taking in Gentiles without circumcision. As yet there had been no mass influx of Gentiles, and the problems were not altogether evident. Things would change, particularly with the great success of Paul and Barnabas's mission among the Gentiles. Once again the issue would be raised by the more staunchly Jewish faction— "Shouldn't Gentiles be circumcised when they become Christians?" "Can we really have table fellowship with uncircumcised Gentiles who do not abide by the food laws?" . . . These issues would surface once more for a final showdown in the Jerusalem Conference of [chapter] 15.[4]

## The Jerusalem Council

The threat to church unity faced by early Christians was real and difficult to face. Jewish Christians thought salvation was possible only for those who belonged to the covenant people of God, inferring that circumcision was a requirement. And, as part of a faithful lifestyle, Christian Jews also believed they were to avoid contact with Gentiles that could possibly thwart their own salvation. Eating with Gentiles and sinners was thus forbidden.

Jews had very strict laws to regulate their association with Gentiles. These regulations quickly became a stumbling block for the new Christian community when the apostles began to reach out to Gentiles who wished to become followers of Jesus. Since the Messiah is the Savior of God's covenant people as predicted in the Old Testament, weren't Gentiles desiring salvation required to become Jews and follow the rules of the covenant?

That this issue was not only a cultural matter is evident from the discussion. It was rooted in conflict over deeply held interpretations of the Old Testament stories regarding circumcision and relationship with Gentiles. As apostles, elders, and delegates from Antioch sat together, it seems the discussion continued for a long time without any resolution. In fact, it appears the discussion was quite heated. Nevertheless, toward the end of this passionate debate, three apostles, Peter, Barnabas, and Paul, made speeches that finally brought light and resolution. Their speeches have common elements as they share with the assembly their testimonies of how the Holy Spirit worked through them to bring about the conversion of Gentiles. Their stories of miracles and wonders among the Gentiles give evidence of the Holy Spirit's work. They conclude by saying, "We believe that through the grace of the Lord Jesus Christ we shall be saved in the same manner as they" (Acts 15:11). And that's the clinching argument of this discussion. The Holy Spirit had guided their experiences and ministries to a new reality, a Bible truth they had not seen before.

## A difficult solution

After hours of discussion between the apostles and elders, James, the brother of Jesus, who appears to be the leader of the assembly, offered his opinion and decision on a way forward. In convincing fashion, the council decided that Gentiles do not need to become Jewish converts, obeying all aspects of the ceremonial laws, including circumcision, in order to be recipients of God's salvation.

James quotes from Amos 9:11, 12 in his decision to allow Gentiles into the Christian community, and we see allusions to the salvation of the nations in other Old Testament prophets (Isaiah 42:1). It was God's intention all along to save the entire world through Israel's witness and experience. In fact, God's call to Abraham included a blessing for all nations through him and his descendants (Genesis 17:4).[5]

Although these prophecies had been read many times, Jews had not been able to foresee their fulfillment. The leading of the Holy Spirit, the ministry of Peter, Barnabas, and Paul among the Gentiles, and the conversion of many Gentiles were confirmations that could not be set aside. These testimonies helped leaders of the Christian community in Jerusalem realize that many Old Testament prophecies were now being fulfilled. God had already given laws guiding the presence of Gentiles in Israel and what restrictions applied to them (Leviticus 17, 18). James also referred to these laws in his decision (Acts 15:29). It became obvious to everyone that God was calling Gentiles to join His people and receive salvation in Jesus. The guidance of the Holy Spirit made possible a new understanding of Scripture and key passages that applied to Gentiles, passages that had previously been dimly understood.

After many days of discussion, testimony from apostles and Gentiles, and guidance of the Holy Spirit, the early church found scriptural support for welcoming Gentiles into the Christian community. The church was strengthened and a major schism averted. Of course, this result required a level of trust from the church at Antioch when it sent representatives to Jerusalem to seek counsel with other apostles and elders.

They trusted that together they would find the best solution to their conflict.

These stories in the book of Acts teach us that church unity is rooted in a mind-set of trust, confidence, and love for one another. The influence of the Holy Spirit brought humble acceptance of positions that appeared to contradict long-held interpretations of Scripture, producing a revolutionary solution and bringing greater unity in purpose and mission.

---

1. The Greek widows are likely not Gentiles, and these two groups are both Jewish and believers in Jesus, the Messiah. One is from the Jewish diaspora and speaks Greek, and the other is from Judea and speaks Aramaic. The first Gentiles to become believers in Jesus are Cornelius and his household in Acts 10. Mikeal C. Parsons, *Acts*, Paideia: Commentaries on the New Testament (Grand Rapids, MI: Baker Academic, 2008), 82.

2. Ellen G. White, *The Acts of the Apostles* (Mountain View, CA: Pacific Press®, 1911), 88.

3. Denis Fortin, "Life Together and Conflict Resolution," *Ministry: International Journal for Pastors* 90, no. 2 (February 2018): 16, 17.

4. John B. Polhill, *Acts*, The New American Commentary (Nashville, TN: Broadman Press, 1992), 268.

5. In the Septuagint, the Greek translation of the Old Testament, the word "nation" (*ethnos*) is used to refer to the nations that God would bless through Abraham (Genesis 17:4) and that would accept His salvation (Isaiah 42:1; Amos 9:12). This word is also translated "Gentiles" and is thus part of the argument used by the apostles and James.

# Unity in Faith

The decades of the 1880s and 1890s showed a darker side of Seventh-day Adventism and a tendency to internal conflict. Intense friction over the interpretation of secondary biblical concepts reached its climax in 1888 during a General Conference session in Minneapolis, Minnesota. While pastors and church leaders were debating the identity of the ten horns of the prophecy of Daniel 7 and of the law in Galatians 3:24, few realized how their hostile attitudes toward each other destroyed their fellowship and friendship, thus marring the unity and mission of the church.

Ellen White, who attended the conference, deeply deplored this state of affairs and encouraged those involved in these debates to think carefully about their relationship with Jesus and consider how His love should be demonstrated to one another. She also indicated we should not expect everyone in the church to agree on every point of interpretation. She said it is natural to have diversity of thought on some issues, but in 1905 she also emphasized that we should seek unity of understanding when it comes to core beliefs. "Let the truths that are the foundation of our faith be kept before the people."[1]

The written Word of God, the Bible, and the incarnate Word of God, Jesus, are closely connected in Scripture and naturally bring convictions that flow from Scripture. These convictions consist of a common and unique body of beliefs that constitute an important unifying element within the Seventh-day Adventist Church. God's end-time people have much in common with other Christian bodies, and yet our set of beliefs form a unique system of biblical truth. In this chapter we will examine four core Adventist beliefs that bring meaning to our unity in faith.

### Salvation in Jesus

In response to a question from the Sanhedrin as to who gave Peter and John the power to heal a crippled man, Peter responded that their power came from Jesus of Nazareth and that there is "no other name under heaven given among men by which we must be saved" (Acts 4:12). And later to Cornelius, Peter also said, "To Him [Jesus] all the prophets witness that, through His name, whoever believes in Him will receive remission of sins" (Acts 10:43).

Adventists unequivocally affirm that the salvation of humankind is possible only through Jesus Christ. It is with this good news in mind that the apostle Paul told the Corinthians "that God was in Christ reconciling the world to Himself" (2 Corinthians 5:19). Christ's death is the means of our reconciliation with the Father, bridging the chasm left by sin and death. For centuries, Christians have pondered the meaning of Jesus' death, resurrection, and reconciliation that He came to accomplish. This process of reconciliation has been termed "atonement." This old English word originally meant "at-one-ment" and means a state of being "at one," or in agreement. Accordingly, atonement denotes harmony in a relationship that has been previously estranged. Church unity is a result of this reconciliation and flows from the death of Jesus on Calvary.[2]

The meaning of Christ's atonement has multiple biblical nuances, and each of them enhances a fuller understanding of the redemption Jesus has accomplished. When John the Baptist pointed to Jesus of Nazareth as "the Lamb of God who

74

takes away the sin of the world" (John 1:29), he made a clear allusion to the Old Testament sacrificial ceremonies that were intended also as a typology of the future sacrifice of the Messiah. Using sacrificial language from the books of Exodus and Leviticus, the apostles referred to Jesus' death as a propitiatory sacrifice or sacrifice of expiation (1 John 2:2; 4:9, 10). Paul used the word *hilasterion* to refer to Jesus' death as a "sacrifice of atonement" (Romans 3:25, NIV) or "propitiation" (NKJV, NASB). This same word was used in the Greek Septuagint to describe the cover of the ark of the covenant, on which the blood of the goat was sprinkled on the Day of Atonement (Leviticus 16:2, 14; see Hebrews 9:5). The apostle John's use of the cognate word *hilasmos* also refers to the atoning sacrifices in the Old Testament and to the special sacrifices on the Day of Atonement (1 John 2:2; 4:10; Leviticus 25:9). What both Paul and John emphasize is that all people can have their sins forgiven because of the sacrificial death of Christ. He has made the ultimate sacrifice that need not be repeated (Hebrews 7:23–27).

Other concepts mentioned in the New Testament include Jesus suffering on the cross to give us an example to follow in situations of suffering and persecution (1 Peter 2:21–23). Additionally, Peter describes Him as bearing our sins on the cross and dying the death that should have been ours (verse 24). Matthew and Timothy remind first-century Christians that Jesus' death redeemed them from this world of sin (Matthew 20:28; 1 Timothy 2:5, 6). What this means is that Christ's life, death, and resurrection have bridged the chasm of sin, and in Him we have the hope and assurance of eternal life (John 3:16).

In 1866, Samuel J. Stone, an Anglican pastor in Windsor, Berkshire, England, composed a well-known hymn, "The Church Has One Foundation." The inspiration for the hymn came from a phrase in the Apostles' Creed that refers to the church, and the first stanza affirms a foundational statement of the Christian faith—its oneness is built on Christ:

The church has one foundation,
'Tis Jesus Christ her Lord;
She is His new creation,
By water and the word;
From heaven He came and sought her
To be His holy bride;
With His own blood He bought her,
And for her life He died.[3]

### Jesus' ministry in the heavenly sanctuary

Another crucial belief of Seventh-day Adventists concerns the ministry of Jesus in heaven from the time of His ascension to His second coming. In the Old Testament, God instructed Moses to build a tabernacle, or sanctuary, to serve as His dwelling place (Exodus 25:8). This was a place, through its services and ceremonies, where the people of Israel were taught the plan of salvation, and it served as an illustration of Jesus' priestly ministry in heaven.

Since His ascension, the heavenly sanctuary is the place where Christ conducts His priestly ministry for our salvation. Hebrews promises that "He is . . . able to save to the uttermost those who come to God through Him, since He always lives to make intercession for them" (Hebrews 7:25). Therefore, we are encouraged to "come boldly to the throne of grace, that we may obtain mercy and find grace to help in time of need" (Hebrews 4:16). "Christ's current ministry is rooted in His death and resurrection. While the atoning sacrifice at Calvary was sufficient and complete, without the resurrection we would have no assurance that Christ had successfully finished His divine mission on earth."[4]

Thus, we have confidence that Jesus intercedes for us. "But now He has obtained a more excellent ministry, inasmuch as He is also Mediator of a better covenant, which was established on better promises" (Hebrews 8:6). "If we confess our sins, He is faithful and just to forgive us our sins and to cleanse us from all unrighteousness. . . . And if anyone sins, we have an Advocate with the Father, Jesus Christ the righteous. And He

Himself is the propitiation for our sins, and not for ours only but also for the whole world" (1 John 1:9; 2:1, 2).

As the earthly tabernacle had two phases of priestly ministry—first on a daily basis in the Holy Place, and then once a year in the Most Holy Place—the Scriptures also describe these two phases of Jesus' ministry in heaven. His ministry in the Holy Place in heaven is characterized by a ministry of intercession, forgiveness, reconciliation, and restoration. Repentant sinners have immediate access to the Father through Jesus the Mediator (1 Timothy 2:5). Jesus' ministry in the Most Holy Place deals also with the aspects of judgment and cleansing that were done once a year on the Day of Atonement (Leviticus 16). His ministry of cleansing the sanctuary is also based on His shed blood and illustrates the judgment process that deals with the eradication of sin. The atonement performed on the Day of Atonement foreshadowed the final application of the merits of Christ to remove the presence of sin for all eternity and to accomplish the complete reconciliation of the universe into one harmonious government under God.

This ministry of Christ in heaven is meaningful to Christians because it both focuses on the reconciliation He has effected between humanity and the Father and highlights His intercession that enables our personal and community relationships to be reconciled. Any understanding of unity must first focus on what Christ has achieved and continues to accomplish on behalf His people.

### Second coming of Christ

The Bible repeatedly assures us that Jesus will come again to claim His redeemed people. The apostles and early Christians considered Christ's return to be "the blessed hope" (Titus 2:13) and expected all the prophecies of Scripture to be fulfilled at His second advent. Seventh-day Adventists still hold firmly to this conviction. In fact, our name, "Adventist," states it unequivocally! All who love Christ look forward with anticipation to the day when they will be able to enjoy face-to-face fellowship with Him. "Let not your heart be troubled," Jesus said to His disciples on the night He was betrayed, "you believe in God, believe also in Me. In My Father's house are many mansions; if it were not so, I would have told you. I go to prepare a place for you. And if I go and prepare a place for you, I will come again and receive you to Myself; that where I am, there you may be also" (John 14:1–3). This beautiful promise still warms our hearts. And though we have experienced a long delay in the fulfillment of this promise, a vibrant hope in the second coming of Christ is a unifying teaching for God's people.

The New Testament explains that Christ's return will be a personal event and not a spiritual or mystical experience. The angels who saw Jesus ascend to heaven after His resurrection told the disciples that He would come back in the same manner as He ascended to heaven—in a literal, visible manner (Acts 1:11). Elsewhere in the New Testament we are told that all the angels of heaven will accompany Jesus during this momentous event (Revelation 19:11–16).

The timing of Christ's return should not be a matter of concern because He Himself stated, "Of that day and hour no one knows, not even the angels of heaven, but My Father only" (Matthew 24:36). However, this does not mean that Christians should be idle as they wait. The gospel of Matthew recounts that Jesus told five parables to exhort His disciples to vigilance in their personal preparation for His second coming. The first exhortation is built on the imagery of the people in the days of Noah (verses 37–39). In this parable Jesus emphasized that His return would be unexpected and that people would be unaware that a judgment is about to take place.

The second parable about the faithful and wise servant (verses 45–51) made the point that Jesus' disciples should be faithful and responsible to their assigned tasks in the interval between Jesus' resurrection and second coming. The third exhortation in the parable of the ten virgins (Matthew 25:1–13) calls for an ongoing spiritual preparation in expectation of the last judgment. The references to lamps, having sufficient oil, and sleeping during a long delay signal that the Christian experience is not to be based on emotional excitement or enthusiasm but on a continued reliance on the grace of God and faithful perseverance, even when there is no tangible evidence of the fulfillment of God's promises. Jesus still invites us to "watch" and be ready at any time for His coming.

The fourth parable is still another exhortation to faithfulness and making good use of the gifts God has given (verses 14–30). Disciples of Christ are not all gifted alike, but all can wisely use their gifts to God's glory. Though the delay may cause some to wonder about the use of one's gifts, faithful stewards will not be dismayed by this and will continue to act in a responsible and judicious manner. The final exhortation focuses on the judgment of the nations at the second coming of Jesus (verses 31–46). The criteria for judgment in this exhortation emphasizes faithfulness and responsibility while waiting for the return of Christ.

Some have suspected that in these exhortations and parables, along with the Sermon on the Mount (Matthew 5–7), Jesus was teaching a form of salvation by works. But that is not the case. In Matthew 20:1–16, Jesus' teaching in the parable of the workers in the vineyard is framed within the context of grace. The parables and exhortations of Matthew 24 and 25, when properly interpreted, do not support salvation by works. Rather, they show that "judgment is based on one's actions in response to the proclamation of the gospel, because that is a response to Jesus."[5]

Hope in the second coming of Jesus teaches one more important concept on which to focus our common unity in Christ: the hope of the resurrection and the moment when all the redeemed will be reunited. Although people are born mortal and subject to death, the Bible speaks of Jesus Christ as the source of immortality. He gives the promise of immortality and eternal life to all those who believe in His salvation. "The gift of God is eternal life in Christ Jesus our Lord" (Romans 6:23). Jesus "has abolished death and brought life and immortality to light through the gospel" (2 Timothy 1:10). "For God so loved the world that He gave His only begotten Son, that whoever believes in Him should not perish but have everlasting life" (John 3:16). It is abundantly clear: there is hope of life after death.

In 1 Corinthians 15:51–54 and 1 Thessalonians 4:13–18, Paul reminds people that God promises to bestow immortality upon His own at the resurrection, when the last trumpet will sound. While believers receive the promise of eternal life at the moment they accept Jesus as their Savior, immortality is promised at the resurrection. This promise also informs our understanding of church unity and our common future in Christ.

## The Sabbath

Another crucial teaching of Scripture that Seventh-day Adventists uphold with great zeal is the seventh-day Sabbath. This key doctrine strengthens unity and fellowship among us.

The Sabbath is God's gift to humanity right from the days of Creation (Genesis 2:1–3). At Creation, three divine acts established the Sabbath: (1) God rested on the Sabbath, (2) He blessed the day, and (3) He sanctified it. These three divine actions instituted the Sabbath as God's special gift enabling the human race to experience the reality of heaven on earth. A well-known Jewish rabbi, Abraham Joshua Heschel, has called the Sabbath "a palace in time," a holy day when God meets with His people.[6]

Desiring to follow Jesus' example, Seventh-day Adventists customarily observe the Sabbath just as Jesus did (Luke 4:16). His participation in Sabbath services reveals that He endorsed it as a day of rest and worship. Some of His miracles were done on the Sabbath to teach that healing (both physical and spiritual) comes from the celebration of the Sabbath (see Luke 13:10–17). The apostles and early Christians understood that Jesus had not abolished the Sabbath. They kept it as well and attended worship on that day (Acts 13:14, 42, 44; 16:13; 17:2; 18:4).

There are seven broad dimensions of the meaning of the Sabbath for humanity that Seventh-day Adventists teach. These dimensions are most valuable when we speak of unity.

First, the Sabbath is a perpetual memorial of God's creation (Genesis 2:1–3; Exodus 20:8–11) and His personal involvement in the creation of humankind. The observance of the Sabbath serves as a reminder of our common heritage.

Another beautiful dimension of the Sabbath is the symbol of redemption. It is the memorial of God's salvation of the people of Israel from slavery in Egypt (Deuteronomy 5:12–15) and by extension, it symbolizes humanity's salvation from the slavery of sin. A third important dimension is the aspect of God's transforming power; the Sabbath is a sign of holiness and sanctification (Exodus 31:13). "Just as God has set the Sabbath aside for a holy purpose, so He has set His people apart for a holy purpose—to be His special witnesses. Their communion with Him on that day leads to holiness; they learn to depend not on their own resources but on the God who sanctifies them."[7]

The Sabbath also signifies loyalty in that it is the only commandment that names the name of God (Exodus 20:10, 11; Deuteronomy 5:12–15; Ezekiel 20:12). Obedience to this commandment brings one into direct relationship with the God of creation. A fifth dimension is fellowship: fellowship with one another and with God. Since it is a day of rest, it gives the blessed opportunity to rest from busy schedules and focus on meaningful relationships. The Sabbath, therefore, "provides time to commune with God through worship, prayer, song, the study of and meditation on the Word, and sharing the gospel with others. The Sabbath is our opportunity to experience God's presence."[8]

The Sabbath is a sign of righteousness by faith and of our salvation by grace. In observing the Sabbath, believers are not trying to make themselves righteous. Rather, respect for this day flows from a relationship with Christ as Creator and Redeemer. By observing this day of rest, "believers reveal a willingness to accept God's will for their lives instead of depending on their own judgment."[9] For that reason, one should be careful not to portray restrictions of activities on the Sabbath as a means of gaining God's favor with those who are more careful in its observance. Such an approach to Sabbath observance invariably leads to salvation by works.

One last dimension is rest in Christ. As the Sabbath is a sign of deliverance from sin, it is also a sign of rest and salvation in Christ. Despite Israel's failure to fully enter this rest because of repeated disobedience and idolatry, God still promises that "there remains therefore a rest for the people of God" (Hebrews 4:9). All who desire to enter this rest can do so by placing their faith in the salvation Jesus provides. No need to wait for the peace, grace, and joy Jesus offers. You can have it now. The observance and celebration of the Sabbath symbolizes this spiritual rest in Christ and reliance on His merits to save us from sin and give us the hope of eternal life. "For he who has entered His rest has himself also ceased from his works as God did from His" (verse 10; see also Matthew 11:28–30).

Understood in this context, the Sabbath is a divine concept of unity centered on God's creation and His redemption of humanity. As such, it provides an unparalleled opportunity to experience unity and fellowship with other Christians.

1. Ellen G. White, *Counsels to Writers and Editors* (Nashville, TN: Southern Publishing Association, 1946), 29.

2. *Seventh-day Adventists Believe . . . : A Biblical Exposition of Fundamental Doctrines*, 2nd ed. (Silver Spring, MD: Ministerial Association, General Conference of Seventh-day Adventists, 2005), 125.

3. *The Seventh-day Adventist Church Hymnal* (Washington, DC: Review and Herald®, 1985), no. 348. Public domain.

4. *Seventh-day Adventists Believe*, 130.

5. Charles H. Talbert, *Matthew*, Paideia: Commentaries on the New Testament (Grand Rapids, MI: Baker Academic, 2010), 277.

6. Abraham Joshua Heschel, *The Sabbath: Its Meaning for Modern Man* (New York: The Noonday Press, 1951), 13–24.

7. *Seventh-day Adventists Believe*, 288, 289.

8. *Seventh-day Adventists Believe*, 289.

9. *Seventh-day Adventists Believe*, 290.

CHAPTER

# The Most
# Convincing Proof

In a short document written in 1903, Ellen White commented on Jesus' words in John 17:20–23, "Unity with Christ establishes a bond of unity with one another. This unity is the most convincing proof to the world of the majesty and virtue of Christ, and of His power to take away sin."[1] In the last chapter, we studied how unity is made visible through a common unifying message, centered on Jesus as Savior and on the truths of Scripture. In this chapter, we focus on the visible unity of the church in the day-to-day lives of Christians and the mission of the church community.

According to Jesus, the church does not simply proclaim God's message of salvation—it lives the gospel when it expresses unity in its daily life. That is to say, in a world surrounded by sin and rebellion, the church stands as a visible witness to the saving work and power of Christ to bring an end to the divisiveness of sin. Without oneness and solidarity in the church, its witness to the saving power of the Cross would hardly be apparent to the world. We often hear the expression that a picture is worth a thousand words. So it is with the church—its visible expression of unity and solidarity speaks volumes to an onlooking world. In Christ, we can thus show unity to the world and witness to our common faith in tangible ways. There are important biblical concepts in the New Testament that show how the Christian community can make its visible witness more powerful.

### Under the cross of Jesus

From a practical standpoint, is unity something to be produced by churches through tireless efforts at reconciliation? To some extent, of course, churches have to work on unity, but like many other spiritual blessings God gives His people, church unity is also a gift. Unity is not a human creation brought about through efforts, good works, and grand intentions—although all these are necessary. Fundamentally, Jesus Christ creates unity through His death and resurrection. By faith, as we appropriate His death and resurrection through baptism and the forgiveness of sin, we enter into union with Him and one another. Church unity is first and foremost a spiritual condition bestowed through faith in Christ.

Two key passages of the New Testament affirm this concept of unity in the death of Christ. When plotting to kill Jesus, members of the Jerusalem Sanhedrin heard Caiaphas state prophetically that it was better for one man, Jesus, to die in order to avert the persecution of the Jewish people at the hands of the dreaded Romans. The apostle John makes this observation, "Now this he did not say on his own authority; but being high priest that year he prophesied that Jesus would die for the nation, and not for that nation only, but also that He would gather together in one the children of God who were scattered abroad" (John 11:51, 52). "The evangelist discerned in the high priest's pronouncement a deeper meaning, unknown to Caiaphas himself, that enunciated an important divine truth related to the nature of Jesus' cross-death. Whereas Caiaphas thinks on a 'purely political level, John invites his readers to think in terms of the Lamb of God who takes away the sin of the world.'" Jesus' death anticipates the gathering of the nations and their unity in Him (see also John 10:14–16).[2] And in the epistle to the Ephesians, Paul asserts "that in the dispensation of the fullness of the times He [God] might gather together in one all things in Christ" (Ephesians 1:10).

A key thought from both John and Paul in these two passages is the impact of Christ's death on the unity of those who accept His death for their salvation, the Christian community of believers. It is clear that unity is created by Jesus' death and a common faith in His redemption. And, furthermore, Christians also experience this unity in Christ through baptism. "You are all sons of God through faith in Christ Jesus. For as many of you as were baptized into Christ have put on Christ" (Galatians 3:26, 27). Baptism is another bond that symbolizes faith in Christ. All born-again and baptized believers share a common relationship in Him. This bond is the foundation of unity. Christians have a common Father—they are all sons and daughters of God—and have a common Savior in whose death and resurrection they are baptized (Romans 6:3, 4). This biblical concept is crucial and foundational for any visible unity and witness.

### Ministry of reconciliation

Our lives are touched by the disorders, troubles, and wars and conflicts with which we live. All of these factors affect us at the personal, communal, and national levels—even in the church. At times, it appears our entire lives are in conflict, but the Bible promises that disunity and disorder will not prevail forever. God is on a mission to bring about cosmic unity. Whereas sin has resulted in disharmony, God's eternal plan for reconciliation brings peace and wholeness. As Christians genuinely live out their faith, reconciliation becomes a visible demonstration of a shared unity in Christ. In the ministry of reconciliation, Christians share and participate in God's mission on earth.

As noted in chapter 7, early Christians experienced tension between ethnic groups. Social walls of separation between them were natural and rose without much effort. But the essence of God's plan of salvation in Christ had a different set of references for the church. In Ephesians 2, Paul stressed that in Christ walls of separation are set aside, that Christ "might reconcile them both [Jews and Gentiles] to God in one body through the cross, thereby putting to death the enmity" (verse 16).

In proclaiming Christ as our peace (verse 17), Paul also put forward principles that show how Christ acted to bring peace: through His death on the cross He made both Jews and Gentiles one people and destroyed the ethnic and religious barriers that separated them. If Christ was able to do this with Jews and Gentiles in the first century, can He still bring down racial, ethnic, and cultural barriers that divide people within the church today? Undoubtedly, He can!

In 2 Corinthians 5:17–21, Paul stated that in Christ we are new creations, reconciled to God. As God's new creations, believers receive a threefold ministry of reconciliation. First, the church is composed of believers who were once alienated from God but through the saving grace of Christ's sacrifice have now been united to God by the Holy Spirit. We are God's chosen people and His family. Our ministry is to invite those who are still alienated from God to be reconciled to Him. Second, the church is also God's people reconciled to one another. To be united to Christ means we are united to fellow believers. This is not only a spiritual philosophy; it must be a visible reality. Reconciliation that brings peace and harmony among brothers and sisters is an unmistakable witness to the world that Jesus Christ is our Savior and Redeemer. "By this all will know that you are My disciples, if you have love for one another," Jesus said in the gospel of John (John 13:35).

Third, through this ministry of reconciliation, the church tells the universe that God's plan of redemption is true and powerful. The great controversy between good and evil is about God and His character, and when the church cultivates unity and reconciliation, the universe sees the outworking of God's eternal wisdom (see Ephesians 3:8–11). David Garland comments perceptively that "the ministry of reconciliation therefore involves more than simply explaining to others what God has done in Christ. It requires that one become an active reconciler oneself. Like Christ, a minister of reconciliation plunges into the midst of human tumult to bring harmony out of chaos, reconciliation out of estrangement, and love in the place of hate."[3]

### The example of Jesus

Perhaps the most winsome approach to unity is to reflect the example of Jesus in our lives and relationships with others. In 1902, Ellen White wrote this insightful comment, "What Christ was in His life on this earth, that every Christian is to be. He is our example, not only in His spotless purity, but in His patience, gentleness, and winsomeness of disposition."[4] These words are reminiscent of Paul's appeal to the Philippians: "Let this mind be in you which was also in Christ Jesus" (Philippians 2:5). This is an important theme of New Testament life in Christ.

Many other scriptures invite Christians to follow Jesus' example be living witnesses to God's grace. We are invited to seek the welfare of others (Matthew 7:12); to bear each other's burdens (Galatians 6:2); to live in simplicity and focus on inward spirituality instead of outward display (Matthew 16:24–26; 1 Peter 3:3, 4); to follow healthy living practices (1 Corinthians 10:31); and to have lives committed to helping others in simple and unassuming ways (Matthew 25:40).

To the Ephesians, Paul raised a very high standard of living. At the end of Ephesians 4, he counseled them to be careful and kind in their relationships with others and then concluded, "Therefore be imitators of God as dear children" (Ephesians 5:1). To the Colossians, he stated something similar. "If then you were raised with Christ, seek those things which are above, where Christ is, sitting at the right hand of God. Set your mind on things above, not on things on the earth" (Colossians 3:1, 2). Such an attitude and lifestyle would impact their relationships with others and transform their church life. "Whatever you do in word or deed, do all in the name of the Lord Jesus, giving thanks to God the Father through Him" (verse 17).

The apostle Peter had similar counsel to give. "Beloved, I beg you as sojourners and pilgrims, abstain from fleshly lusts which war against the soul, having your conduct honorable among the Gentiles, that when they speak against you as evildoers, they may, by your good works which they observe, glorify God in the day of visitation" (1 Peter 2:11, 12). How often do we underestimate the impact of Christian character upon those who watch us? The patience manifested in moments of annoyance, a disciplined life in the midst of tension and conflict, a gentle spirit in response to impatient and harsh words, all mark the spirit of Jesus we are invited to emulate. As Christians witness together in a world that misunderstands the character of God, they become a power for good and for His glory. As representatives of Christ, believers are to be known not only for their moral rectitude but also for their practical interest in the welfare of others, even those who are nonbelievers. If our religious experience is genuine, it will reveal itself and impact the world in which we live (see Matthew 5:16). As "sojourners and pilgrims" in a sinful world, Christians can live their lives in a way that makes a difference in their community and effects social change. Such a witness is a result of Christian unity and strengthens unity among believers who share a common goal: to reflect the character of Jesus.

### Unity and tolerance of diversity

In Romans 14 and 15, the apostle Paul addresses issues that were deeply dividing the church at Rome. His response to these issues was to invite the Romans to show tolerance and patience for one another, sparing the church from division over these concerns. Important lessons can be learned from his counsel regarding two matters that divided the community of faith: what to eat or not to eat, and what days to observe as holy days.

We know there were some regulations and restrictions about food and special days in both Roman and Jewish religious customs in the first century. The matters Paul discussed in these chapters likely had to do with religious and ceremonial impurities, which would have prevented some people from fully participating in Christian assemblies. Such an issue is also discussed in Paul's other letters (Galatians 2:11–14; Colossians 2:16–19). According to Paul in Romans 14:1, these matters were "disputes over doubtful things" (NKJV) or "opinions" (NASB), indicating that they were not matters of salvation.

These disputes were first over food and drink. Eating animals forbidden in Leviticus 11 was not the problem Paul addressed. There is no convincing evidence that early Christians began eating pork or other unclean animals during Paul's time, and we know that Peter did not eat any such food (see Acts 10:14). Also, the fact that the "weak brothers" only ate vegetables (Romans 14:2) and that the controversy also involved beverages (verses 17, 21) indicates that the concern focused on ceremonial impurity. This is further evidenced by the word "unclean" (*koinos*) used in Romans 14:14. That word used in the Greek Septuagint translation of the Old Testament referred to impure animals, not the unclean animals of Leviticus 11. An impure animal was a clean animal (according to the regulations of Leviticus 11) that had been either sacrificed to idols, improperly slaughtered, or had been in contact with unclean animals.[5] There were some people in the Roman community who would not eat at fellowship meals because they were not convinced that the food was adequately prepared or might have been sacrificed to idols.

The same goes for the observation of some holy days. Romans had numerous religious days they observed, and some of them were deemed evil or inauspicious by Christians. Jews also had many religious days for fasting, and although the Sabbath is often listed by commentators as one of these days, it is doubtful that Paul included it or had it in mind, since we know he and his colleagues observed it regularly (Acts 13:14; 16:13; 17:2). Nevertheless, the manner of observing the Sabbath as urged by some Romans may have been part of Paul's concern, and we know that this was also a concern Jesus expressed repeatedly in the Gospels (Mark 2:23–28; 3:1–6). The important point for Paul in these verses is his urging to tolerance for those who are sincere and conscientious in the observance of these rituals. Unity among Christians manifests itself in patience and forbearance when we do not exactly agree on the demonstration of our faith and spiritual experience. Thus, there is room for diversity of religious expression. Furthermore, Paul requires a charitable response toward those in the church who, because of different religious and ethnic heritage, wish to worship God differently than the majority.

The principles of tolerance and forbearance we learn from this passage are crucial for church unity. First, Paul asserts that our personal lives are lived in Christ, and that realization will make a difference in interpersonal relationships between brothers and sisters. "For none of us lives to himself, and no one dies to himself. For if we live, we live to the Lord; and if we die, we die to the Lord. Therefore, whether we live or die, we are the Lord's" (Romans 14:7, 8). Paul argues that "if the weak and the strong remember that the pattern of their own lives has been determined by the one who is the Lord of the living and the dead, they will set aside their disputes in order to live for him."[6]

From this first principle flows a second. "Do not destroy with your food the one for whom Christ died. Therefore do not let your good be spoken of as evil; for the kingdom of God is not eating and drinking, but righteousness and peace and joy in the Holy Spirit" (Romans 14:15–17). Paul is here defining true purity as inner holiness and righteousness. The Christian life and interpersonal relationships within the community are marked by inner qualities and virtues, rather than strict food regulations and religious rituals.

A third crucial principle for church unity is found in Romans 15:5–7. "Now may the God of patience and comfort grant you to be like-minded toward one another, according to Christ Jesus, that you may with one mind and one mouth glorify the God and Father of our Lord Jesus Christ. Therefore receive one another, just as Christ also received us, to the glory of God." When small matters and secondary opinions threaten our communities, we need to remember that the pattern for our behavior is Jesus Christ. Paul's prayer is that the glory of God will be manifested in the way we relate to one another in Christ. "If the community is divided, there will always be something lacking in its worship."[7]

This transcendent principle is yet another foundational

concept for Christian unity: Paul downplays the importance of personal religious practices for the sake of unity in the body of Christ. One's personal preferences should not be given a level of importance that dominates the shared life of the community.

---

1. Ellen G. White, "That They May Be One; as We Are One," Manuscript 111, 1903, published in Ellen G. White Comments in *Seventh-day Adventist Bible Commentary*, ed. Frank D. Nichol, vol. 5 (Washington, DC: Review and Herald®, 1956), 1148.

2. Andreas J. Köstenberger, *John*, Baker Exegetical Commentary on the New Testament (Grand Rapids, MI: Baker Academic, 2004), 352, 353.

3. David E. Garland, *2 Corinthians*, The New American Commentary (Nashville: Broadman & Holman Publishers, 1999), 291, 292.

4. Ellen G. White, "The Grace of Courtesy," *Signs of the Times*, July 16, 1902.

5. Note that the vision Peter received in Acts 10:9–16 makes reference to the two kinds of animals: unclean (*akathartos*) and impure (*koinos*). Both in Romans 14 and in Mark 7 the word used to refer to animals is impure (*koinos*), not the word *akathartos* used in the Greek translation of Leviticus 11 to categorize some animals as unclean. Bible translations often do not make this distinction and translate both words as unclean.

6. Frank J. Matera, *Romans*, Paideia: Commentaries on the New Testament (Grand Rapids, MI: Baker Academic, 2010), 313.

7. Matera, *Romans*, 322.

CHAPTER

# Unity and Broken Relationships

The record shows that even after Pentecost, the relationship between believers in the early church was occasionally strained.[1] The New Testament notes repeated examples of church leaders and individual members dealing with challenges. Their approach to problem-solving is valuable for today's church and demonstrates the positive impact of using biblical principles to deal with conflict in an effort to preserve oneness in Christ.

This chapter focuses on restored relationships and how human relationships impact unity in Christ. The ministry of the Holy Spirit involves bringing people closer to God and to one another. It includes breaking down the barriers that hinder relationships with God and with one another. In short, the greatest demonstration of the power of the gospel is not necessarily what the church says, but how the church lives. "By this all will know that you are My disciples, if you have love for one another" (John 13:35). Without this love, all talk about church unity comes to nothing.

### Restored friendship
In Acts 13, Paul and Barnabas set out on their first missionary journey in their witness for Jesus. Before they left Antioch, John Mark joined the team. Yet after a few weeks of activities,

the potential dangers of preaching the gospel caused John Mark to desert Paul and Barnabas and return home (Acts 13:13). Ellen White comments that "this desertion caused Paul to judge Mark unfavorably, and even severely, for a time. Barnabas, on the other hand, was inclined to excuse him because of his inexperience. He felt anxious that Mark should not abandon the ministry, for he saw in him qualifications that would fit him to be a useful worker for Christ."[2]

When the time came for Paul and Barnabas to begin their second missionary journey, they experienced a "sharp disagreement" (Acts 15:39, NIV) over whether they could trust John Mark again. While Barnabas wished to give him a second chance, Paul was not so willing. Although God used all these men in the proclamation of the gospel, this issue between them needed resolution. The best solution, it was decided, was for them to divide their efforts. Barnabas took John Mark and went back to the island of Cyprus. Paul took Silas as his companion and went to visit the churches in Syria and Cilicia (verses 39–41).

Years later though, it seems that Paul came to a different conclusion about John Mark's usefulness to the gospel ministry. The apostle who preached grace needed to extend grace to a young preacher who had disappointed him. The apostle of forgiveness needed to forgive. John Mark grew under the affirming mentorship of Barnabas, and eventually, Paul's heart was apparently touched by the changes.

Although details of Paul's reconciliation with John Mark are sketchy, the biblical record is clear—John Mark became one of the apostle's trusted companions. Paul highly recommended John Mark as a "fellow worker" to the church at Colossae (Colossians 4:10, 11). At the end of Paul's life, he encouraged Timothy to bring John Mark with him to Rome because he was "useful to me for ministry" (2 Timothy 4:11). Paul's ministry was enriched by the younger preacher, whom he had obviously forgiven. The barrier between them was broken, and they were able to work together in the cause of the gospel. This story teaches that we can, and should, forgive those who hurt or disappoint us. Although we have no evidence of a restored relationship between Paul and Barnabas, we know Paul had a change of heart.

As noted in an earlier chapter, the church at Corinth had many difficult problems, and in his two epistles to the Corinthians, Paul outlined principles for healing and restoring broken relationships. In these passages, the apostle identified critical principles for church unity. He pointed out that Jesus used different workers to accomplish different ministries in His church, even though each one is laboring differently for the building of God's kingdom (1 Corinthians 3:9).

According to Paul, God calls believers to cooperation, not competition. Each one is gifted by Him to cooperate in ministering to the body of Christ and serving the community (1 Corinthians 12:11). There are no greater or lesser gifts, and all gifts are necessary in Christ's church (verses 18–23). Our God-given gifts are not for selfish display since they are given by the Holy Spirit for service. In the end, this is likely what Paul realized in his attitude toward John Mark. God helped him understand that workers in God's church have different gifts for different purposes, but all for God's glory.

### From slave to son

Relationships mattered to Paul. The apostle knew that fractured relationships are detrimental to spiritual growth and church unity. While he was imprisoned in Rome, he met a runaway slave named Onesimus who had fled from Colossae to Rome. Coincidentally, Paul realized he personally knew Onesimus's master, Philemon. The letter to Philemon is Paul's appeal to his friend regarding the need for a restored relationship with the runaway slave. Philemon was a church leader in Colossae, and if he harbored bitterness toward Onesimus, it would color his Christian witness and the witness of the church to the nonbelieving community.

The epistle to Philemon is an intimate letter. At first glance it is somewhat surprising that Paul did not speak more forcefully against the evils of slavery. But Paul's intent was not what we would be concerned with, and in the end his approach proved far more effective. The gospel, ultimately, breaks down all class distinctions (Galatians 3:28; Colossians 3:10, 11). The apostle sent Onesimus back to Philemon, not as a slave but as his spiritual son in Jesus and as Philemon's "beloved brother" in the Lord (Philemon 16). Paul's appeal eventually moved the social status of slaves to one of acceptance and equality in Christ.

Paul knew that runaway slaves had little future and, if discovered, could be apprehended. They were doomed to a life of destitution and poverty. But now, as Philemon's brother in Christ and willing worker, Onesimus could have a good future. His food, lodging, and job could be made secure under Philemon. The restoration of a broken relationship would make a dramatic difference in his life. In his letter to the Colossians, Paul stated that Onesimus had become a "faithful and beloved brother" and co-laborer in the gospel (Colossians 4:9). A common relationship in Christ has a definite impact on personal relationships within the body of Christ (see Galatians 3:28), and the restoration of this broken relationship had a tremendous impact on the life of the early church, ultimately leading to the abolition of slavery in the Western world.

A church that is conscious of how Christ transforms human relationships will live a new pattern of life. To the Colossians, Paul explained what this new pattern looks like. In Christ, human relationships feature kindness, humility, patience, forgiveness, and love (Colossians 3:12–14). "In this passage Paul defines Christian character rather than prescribes rules to obey. For him, morality is a matter of what sort of person one becomes in Christ, where one 'puts on' the capacity for doing the good that God has willed. *Therefore*, believers are transformed by the working of divine grace into people who have the character to do God's will."[3] These Christian qualities are the basis of all conflict resolution and healing of broken relationships. Christian unity is a result of the living presence of Christ and His divine qualities in human hearts.

## Forgiveness and restoration

When it comes to broken relationships and restoring the bonds of fellowship, it is important to consider the divine attribute of forgiveness. But what is forgiveness? Does it justify the behavior of someone who has horribly wronged us? Is my forgiveness dependent on the offender's repentance? What if the one with whom I am upset does not deserve my forgiveness? Many passages of Scripture help us understand the nature of forgiveness.

First, we learn that God took the initiative in reconciling us to Himself. Paul said that it is the "goodness of God [that] leads you to repentance" (Romans 2:4). In Christ, we were reconciled to God while we were yet sinners (Romans 5:8). Thus, our repentance and confession do not create reconciliation; Christ's death on the cross did. Our part is to accept what has been done for us.

It is also true we cannot receive the blessings of forgiveness until we confess our own sins. Jesus asked us to do this in His model prayer (Matthew 6:12, 14, 15). This does not mean our confession creates forgiveness in God's heart. Forgiveness was in His heart all the time. Confession, instead, enables us to receive His forgiveness (1 John 1:9). Confession is vitally important, not because it changes God's attitude toward us but because it changes our attitude toward Him. When we yield to the Holy Spirit's convicting power to repent and confess our sin, we are changed.

Forgiveness is also crucial for our own spiritual well-being. A failure to forgive someone who has wronged us, even if they do not deserve forgiveness, can hurt us more than it hurts them. If an individual has wronged someone and the pain festers inside because we fail to forgive or hold grudges, we are allowing this person to continue to hurt us even more. How often such feelings and hurt are the cause of division and tension in the church. Unresolved hurt between church members damages the unity of the body of Christ. This is what Paul talked about in his letter to the Ephesians. "Let all bitterness, wrath, anger, clamor, and evil speaking be put away from you, with all malice. And be kind to one another, tenderhearted, forgiving one another, even as God in Christ forgave you" (Ephesians 4:31, 32).

Forgiveness, therefore, is releasing another person from our condemnation because Christ has released us from His condemnation. It does not justify another's behavior toward us. We can be reconciled to someone who has wronged us because Christ reconciled us to Himself when we wronged Him. We can forgive because we are forgiven. We can love because we are loved. Forgiveness is a choice. We can choose to forgive in spite of the other person's actions or attitudes. This is the true spirit of Jesus (see Luke 23:34).

Yet, sometimes conflict between brothers and sisters requires more involvement to find a resolution. In Matthew 18:15–17, Jesus gave three simple steps to conflict resolution when one is wronged by another church member. Jesus' desire in giving this counsel was to keep conflict in as small a group as possible. His intent was that the two people involved resolve the problem themselves. This is why Jesus said, "If your brother sins against you, go and tell him his fault between you and him alone" (verse 15). As the number of people involved in a conflict between two individuals increases, contention increases and begins to affect the fellowship of other believers. Often people take sides and battle lines are drawn. But when Christians attempt to settle their differences privately in the spirit of Christian love and mutual understanding, a climate of reconciliation is created. The atmosphere is right for the Holy Spirit to work with them as they strive to resolve their differences.

There are times when personal appeals for conflict resolution are ineffective. In these instances, Jesus invites us to take one or two others with us. This second step in the reconciliation process must always follow the first step. The purpose is to bring people together, not drive them further apart. The one or two who join the offended party are not coming to prove a point or join in blaming the other individual. They come in Christian love and compassion as counselors and prayer partners, ready to participate in the process of bringing two estranged people together.

There are occasions when attempts to solve a problem reach an impasse. In this case, Jesus instructs us to bring the issue before the church. He is certainly not talking about interrupting the weekly worship service with an issue of personal conflict. The appropriate place to bring the issue, if the first two steps have not helped reconcile the two parties, is a private meeting of the church congregation or its administrative council. Again, Christ's purpose on reconciliation is not placing blame on one party and exonerating the other.

The gospel of Jesus Christ is about healing and transformation. Just as our personal lives need God's offer of grace and friendship to bring healing, the same can be said of our community relationships that also need restoration. God is eager to work in and through us to bring healing to all our relationships.

---

1. This chapter is adapted from "Reformation: Healing Broken Relationships," *Adult Sabbath School Bible Study Guide: Revival and Reformation*, July–September 2013, 96–102.

2. Ellen G. White, *The Acts of the Apostles* (Mountain View, CA: Pacific Press®, 1911), 170.

3. Robert W. Wall, *Colossians and Philemon*, The IVP New Testament Commentary Series (Downers Grove, IL: InterVarsity, 1993), 145 (emphasis in the original).

# Unity in Worship

Soon after Pentecost, Luke says, early Christians spent much of their time in worship. "And they continued steadfastly in the apostles' doctrine and fellowship, in the breaking of bread, and in prayers" (Acts 2:42). The joy that came from knowing Jesus as the Messiah, the fulfillment of Old Testament prophecies, filled their hearts with thanksgiving and gratitude to God. These early Christians felt the need for fellowship, study, and prayer. They were grateful for what He had done in their lives and for His revelation in the life, death, and resurrection of Jesus.

They became the church of Jesus Christ, a worshiping community called into being by God to be "a spiritual house, a holy priesthood, to offer up sacrifices acceptable to God through Jesus Christ" (1 Peter 2:5). Gratitude to God expressed in community worship transforms people's hearts and minds into the character of God and prepares them for service. This chapter focuses on the meaning of worship and how it serves to bring unity among believers in Jesus.

### The meaning of worship
Discussions about worship often highlight elements of worship, what it includes and how it is done. But what is the deeper

meaning? What does it mean to worship God? And why do we do it? In Psalm 29:2 David states, "Give unto the LORD the glory due to His name; worship the LORD in the beauty of holiness." This psalm indicates what it means to understand the meaning of worship: to worship the Lord is to give Him the glory and honor He deserves.

In the book of Revelation, chapters 4 and 5 introduce the Lamb of God and Savior of the world through a depiction of worship in the throne room of heaven. This vision shows the inauguration of Jesus in heaven at His ascension, and on that occasion, worship happens when the inhabitants of heaven respond with words of adoration and thankfulness for what He has done (Revelation 5:9, 10, 12, 13). Revelation also depicts the end of time when the redeemed will also join in adoration and respond in a similar way to God's salvation.

> "Great and marvelous are Your works,
> Lord God Almighty!
> Just and true are Your ways,
> O King of the saints!
> Who shall not fear You, O Lord, and glorify Your
>    name?
> For You alone are holy.
> For all nations shall come and worship before You,
> For Your judgments have been manifested" (Revela-
>    tion 15:3, 4).

So worship is a response of our faith in God for His mighty works: first, for creating us and, second, for redeeming us. In worship we give back to God that adoration, reverence, praise, love, and obedience He alone is worthy to receive. Of course, what we know about God, as our Creator and Savior, comes from what He has revealed to us in Scripture. Our knowledge about God is what God said of Himself in the Bible. Furthermore, Christians believe that what we know about God was further, more fully revealed in the person and ministry of Jesus (see John 14:8–14).

# Unity in Worship

This is why Christians worship Jesus as Savior and Redeemer. His sacrificial death and resurrection are at the very core of worship. Robert Rayburn states that "corporate Christian worship is the activity of a congregation of true believers in which they seek to render to God that adoration, praise, confession, intercession, thanksgiving, and obedience to which He is entitled by virtue of the ineffable glory of His person and the magnificent grace of His acts of redemption in Jesus Christ."[1]

When Christians come together in worship, it is out of this sense of awe and thankfulness that worship should proceed. In fact, the apostle Paul goes so far as to say that the entire life of the Christian should be an act of worship. "I beseech you therefore, brethren, by the mercies of God, that you present your bodies a living sacrifice, holy, acceptable to God, which is your reasonable service" (Romans 12:1). What can unite Christians together more than expressing together in worship their appreciation for what God has done? Worship is the greatest expression of unity and the oneness we have in Christ.

Yet, in Western societies, Christian community worship is slowly being forgotten or abandoned. In some countries, less than 15 percent of the population regularly participates in worship. This phenomenon is also affecting Seventh-day Adventist communities. On any given Sabbath in North America, about 50 percent of the Adventist membership is attending worship. While worship is intended to give praise to God for salvation in Christ, it is also a means to create community and fellowship among God's people and nurture their faith. Perhaps broken relationships and lack of unity are symptoms of lower participation rates in worship.

### Elements of Christian worship

Very little is known of the worship practices in early Christian communities, and only a few glimpses are found in the New Testament. There are no suggestions of what a worship service looked like and no descriptions of a liturgy. Yet, we know that early Christians continued many of the same practices used in the Jewish synagogue services. Luke 4 says that Jesus regularly ("as His custom was") went to the synagogue on Sabbath (verse 16). The service included prayers, which were likely a recitation or chanting of the Psalms, and a reading of Scripture passages followed by an exposition of the reading (Luke 4:17; Acts 13:15; 16:13).

Similarly, from the earliest moments of the church, worship has been characterized by the centrality of the study of the Word of God (Acts 2:42). The first Christians were faithful in studying the Scriptures for what it said about Jesus the Messiah and how their lives were changed by this good news. They were in constant fellowship to share with one another the blessings God had given them and to encourage each other in their spiritual walk with God.

Scripture reading and a discussion of its meaning were the most obvious elements of early Christian worship found in the New Testament. Of the many examples given in the book of Acts, the meeting of Paul and Silas with the Bereans is the most notable (Acts 17:10–12). "The minds of the Bereans were not narrowed by prejudice," Ellen White comments. "They were willing to investigate the truthfulness of the doctrines preached by the apostles. They studied the Bible, not from curiosity, but in order that they might learn what had been written concerning the promised Messiah. Daily they searched the inspired records, and as they compared scripture with scripture, heavenly angels were beside them, enlightening their minds and impressing their hearts."[2]

This element of worship is likely what Paul had in mind when he gave this specific instruction to his colleague Timothy. "All Scripture is given by inspiration of God, and is profitable for doctrine, for reproof, for correction, for instruction in righteousness, that the man of God may be complete, thoroughly equipped for every good work. I charge you therefore before God and the Lord Jesus Christ, who will judge the living and the dead at His appearing and His kingdom: Preach the word! Be ready in season and out of season. Convince, rebuke, exhort, with all longsuffering and teaching" (2 Timothy 3:16–4:2).

## Unity in Worship

The study of God's Word forms the core of both worship to God and unity as a people of God. When believers come together as a family to fellowship and worship, God's Word speaks through the scriptures with a call to live for His glory and be prepared for Jesus' second coming. This same Word shapes our unity as we receive the divine instruction to guide our common mission and witness.

Two other elements of early Christian gatherings are the breaking of bread and prayers. "And they continued steadfastly . . . in the breaking of bread, and in prayers" (Acts 2:42). This reference to breaking of bread has been interpreted in two different ways. One is that it simply refers to a fellowship meal or to regular meals shared between believers. Another interpretation refers to the Lord's Supper. At some point during a fellowship meal, someone would offer a special blessing over the bread and wine in memory of Jesus' death and resurrection. Early Christians thus devoted their time to remembering the meaning of Jesus' life and ministry and loved to talk about it in fellowship meals. The meals they shared became moments of worship. "So continuing daily with one accord in the temple, and breaking bread from house to house, they ate their food with gladness and simplicity of heart, praising God and having favor with all the people. And the Lord added to the church daily those who were being saved" (verses 46, 47).

Early Christian worship also included prayer. Right after Jesus' ascension, the early group of disciples "continued with one accord in prayer and supplication" (Acts 1:14). After being forbidden to speak about Jesus by some religious leaders, they prayed and asked God for protection, boldness, and courage (Acts 4:23–31). They prayed for the release of Peter from prison (Acts 12:12), and Paul and Silas prayed even while in prison (Acts 16:25).

The early church cherished the opportunity for direct communication with God and never failed to offer petitions to Him when gathered in worship. Paul in his first epistle to Timothy mentioned the importance of prayer when Christians are together (1 Timothy 2:1). To the Ephesians he also emphasized the need of prayer: "Praying always with all prayer and supplication in the Spirit, being watchful to this end with all perseverance and supplication for all the saints—and for me" (Ephesians 6:18, 19). If worship and prayer had such an impact on the believers in the early church, we should expect the same as we follow in their footsteps.

### Worship and the end time

In contrast to the true worship of our Creator and Savior God, the Scriptures present Satan as seeking to establish a false worship away from the true God and even to secure for himself the adoration and honor due only to God. Whether it is during his confrontation with Jesus in the wilderness (Matthew 4:1–11) or at the end of time (Revelation 13:4), Satan seeks to divert people's attention from God to himself. False worship is a ploy of Satan and will cause many people to be deceived and lose their faith.

The three Hebrew friends in Daniel 3 lived an experience that was in some ways typological of what will happen to God's people in the end time (Revelation 13 and 14). In the heart of Mesopotamia, near the city of Babylon, these Hebrew friends had their faith challenged as well as their determination to worship only the God of their fathers. Their loyalty to God prevented them from giving any consideration to the worship of king Nebuchadnezzar's false idol no matter what the personal consequences might be (Daniel 3:16–18). In the end, God's presence was visibly manifested among them in the fiery furnace, a miracle that even astounded the pagan king (verses 24, 25).

According to Ellen White,

Important are the lessons to be learned from the experience of the Hebrew youth on the plain of Dura. . . .

As in the days of Shadrach, Meshach, and Abednego, so in the closing period of earth's history the Lord will work mightily in behalf of those who stand steadfastly for the right. He who walked with the Hebrew worthies in the fiery furnace will be with His followers wherever they are. His abiding presence will comfort and sustain. In the midst of the time of trouble—trouble such as has not been since there was a nation—His chosen ones will stand unmoved. Satan with all the hosts of evil cannot destroy the weakest of God's saints. Angels that excel in strength will protect them, and in their behalf Jehovah will reveal Himself as a 'God of gods,' able to save to the uttermost those who have put their trust in Him.[3]

Seventh-day Adventists have understood the three angels' messages of Revelation 14:6–12 as depicting God's end-time message just before the second coming of Jesus (Revelation 14:14–20). These important messages, centered on worship, are to be proclaimed with "a loud voice" to all inhabitants of the earth (verses 6, 7).

These angels symbolically proclaim messages to the entire world. This is the fulfillment of Jesus' prediction in Matthew 24:14 that the gospel would be preached to the entire world before His return. There is a sense of urgency and haste in the depiction of these three angels and their mission. The first message urges people to focus on God, as if they had forgotten about Him, because "the hour of His judgment has come." The second coming of Jesus is the catalyst for the judgment.

The call "Fear God" (Revelation 14:7) will generate fear in minds of many, but for those who have been followers of Jesus, this call invites awe and respect. They look up to God and see the fulfillment of His promises. A sense of grateful reverence for His providence overtakes them.

"And worship Him who made heaven and earth, the sea and springs of water" (verse 7). This language is an unmistakable allusion to the Sabbath commandment's reference to Creation (see Exodus 20:8–11). The God of Creation who instituted the Sabbath as a memorial of His creative power is the One who is to be worshiped and revered. It is important to note that at the end of time, worship is the key issue in the great controversy.

In the epic struggle for the allegiance of the human race, this worldwide announcement is a call to worship the Creator.

In this regard, Ranko Stefanovic argues,

> The central issue in the final crisis will be worship. Revelation makes clear that the test will not be denial of worship, but rather who is worshiped. At the time of the end, only two groups of people will be in the world: those who fear and worship the true God (Revelation 11:1, 18; 14:7) and those who hate the truth and are worshipers of the dragon and the beast (Revelation 13:4-8; 14:9-11). . . .
>
> If worship is the central issue in the final conflict, no wonder then that God sends his end-time gospel urging the inhabitants of the earth to take him seriously and worship him as the Creator, the only One worthy of worship.[4]

Seventh-day Adventists have argued that God's commandment to remember and observe the Sabbath is a weekly reminder of God's power in His acts of creation and redemption—which keeps ever present the true reason why worship is due God. Adventist pioneer J. N. Andrews argued that "the Sabbath therefore lies at the very foundation of divine worship, for it teaches this great truth in the most impressive manner, and no other institution does this. The true ground of divine worship, not of that on the seventh day merely, but of all worship, is found in the distinction between the Creator and his creatures. This great fact can never become obsolete, and must never be forgotten."[5]

And Ellen White also endorsed this concept.

> It was to keep this truth ever before the minds of men, that God instituted the Sabbath in Eden; and so long as the fact that He is our Creator continues to be a reason why we should worship Him, so long the Sabbath will continue as its sign and memorial. Had the

Sabbath been universally kept, man's thoughts and affections would have been led to the Creator as the object of reverence and worship, and there would never have been an idolater, an atheist, or an infidel. The keeping of the Sabbath is a sign of loyalty to the true God, "Him that made heaven, and earth, and the sea, and the fountains of waters." It follows that the message which commands men to worship God and keep His commandments will especially call upon them to keep the fourth commandment.[6]

Since the biblical concepts of worship, creation, and salvation are so closely entwined, Adventists have seen the celebration of the Sabbath as God's antidote to false worship. The New Testament makes it clear that true worship is the expression of the Christian believer's gratitude for God's gift of salvation. Without this sincere worship, the community of faith will fail to experience oneness in Christ because this shared experience is the bond of unity and fellowship.

1. Robert G. Rayburn, *O Come, Let Us Worship: Corporate Worship in the Evangelical Church* (Grand Rapids, MI: Baker Book House, 1980), 21.

2. Ellen G. White, *The Acts of the Apostles* (Mountain View, CA: Pacific Press®, 1911), 231.

3. Ellen G. White, *Prophets and Kings* (Mountain View, CA: Pacific Press®, 1943), 512, 513.

4. Ranko Stefanovic, *Revelation of Jesus Christ: Commentary on the Book of Revelation* (Berrien Springs, MI: Andrews University Press, 2002), 444, 445.

5. J. N. Andrews, *History of the Sabbath and First Day of the Week,* Adventist Pioneer Library (Jasper, OR: Light Bearers Ministry, 2015), 431, 432.

6. Ellen G. White, *The Great Controversy* (Mountain View, CA: Pacific Press®, 1911), 438.

# Church Organization and Unity

Large and small organizations know that when employees share a common mission, the company is likely to prosper and become a leader in its field. Such a strategy has turned small businesses into giant enterprises that employ thousands of people. A successful company is one that has visionary leaders who can motivate and empower colleagues to reach new levels of excellence.

The same goes for the church of Christ and its mission. Jesus founded the church for the purpose of spreading the gospel to the entire world. To this end, organization is important because it solidifies and enables the mission of the church. Without church organization, Jesus' saving message could not be as effectively communicated to a dying world. Church leaders are important because they foster unity and exemplify the life of Jesus. In this chapter, we will examine church organization and discover why it is crucial for mission and church unity.

### Christ, the head of the church

As we have already seen, the New Testament church is represented by the metaphor of the body—the church is the body of Christ. This metaphor alludes to several aspects of the church and the relationship between Christ and His people. As the body of Christ, the church depends on Him for its very existence. He is the head (Colossians 1:18; Ephesians 1:22) and the source of the life. Without Him, there would be no church.

In Ephesians 5:23–27, Paul uses the relationship between Christ and His church to illustrate the kind of relationship there should be between husband and wife. Among the key ideas are Christ as the head and Savior of the church, the One who loves the church and gave Himself for her. He also sanctifies and cleanses the church by His word, a reference to the guidance and correction provided by Scripture. These principles are part of Christ's broad and glorious vision for the church, a church He is preparing for eternal life.

The church also derives its identity from Christ. Creeds, beliefs, rituals, and ceremonies do not define the church. It is Christ and His word as revealed in Scripture that determine the nature of the church. Thus, the church derives its identity and significance from Christ. The church has meaning because of who Jesus is, not because of its leaders, however good and wise they may be, nor because of the members and their actions, however noble they may be.

What is abundantly clear is that the church is to be subordinated to the head, Christ, and subject to His authority. "Recognizing that Christ's authority in the church is supreme prevents us from exaggerating the importance of any church official or organizational structure. The church needs organization, of course, but no organizational structure should obscure Christ's authority."[1] There is only one head to the church, and that head is Christ. No human being is to think or pretend to be the head of the church.

Although Jesus' words in Matthew 16:18 ("And I also say to you that you are Peter, and on this rock I will build My church.") have been debated for centuries, both Peter and Paul have said unequivocally that this rock is none other than Jesus (Acts 4:11, 12; 1 Peter 2:4-8, 1 Corinthians 3:11; 10:4).[2]

Since the church is a human organization, with human leaders and human organizational structures, it is tempting to promote a human being as its leader. But to give a person uncritical power, authority, and influence is an enticement that must be resisted. It is important to remember that

> the church is built upon Christ as its foundation; it is to obey Christ as its head. It is not to depend upon man, or be controlled by man. Many claim that a position of trust in the church gives them authority to dictate what other men shall believe and what they shall do. This claim God does not sanction. The Saviour declares, "All ye are brethren." All are exposed to temptation, and are liable to error. Upon no finite being can we depend for guidance. The Rock of faith is the living presence of Christ in the church. Upon this the weakest may depend, and those who think themselves the strongest will prove to be the weakest, unless they make Christ their efficiency.[3]

## Servant leadership

During His earthly ministry, Jesus repeatedly experienced moments when He felt exasperated with His disciples' envy for power. The apostles appeared to be anxious to become powerful leaders in His kingdom (Mark 9:33, 34; Luke 9:46). Even as they were eating their last supper together, these feelings of domination and supremacy were palpably felt among them (Luke 22:24).

On one such occasion, Jesus expressed His thoughts regarding spiritual leadership among His people. The principles of leadership we learn from Jesus' exhortation in Matthew 20:25–28 are crucial for today's church. Darius Jankiewicz argues that "Jesus presents us with two models of authority. The first is the Roman idea of authority. In this model, the elite stand hierarchically over others. They have the power to make decisions and expect submission from those below them. Jesus clearly rejected this model of authority when He stated, 'Not so with you!' Instead He presented the disciples with a breathtakingly new model of authority, a thorough rejection, or reversal, of the hierarchical model with which they were familiar."[4]

The concept of authority that Jesus presents in this anecdote is based on two key words: "servant" (*diakonos*) and "slave" (*doulos*). In some translations the first word, *servant*, is often translated "minister," and the second, "servant" or "bond-servant." Both translations lose much of the force of Jesus' intent. Although He did not wish to abolish all authority structures, He did want to emphasize that church leaders must first of all be servants and slaves of God's people. Their positions are not granted to exercise authority over people, and much less to give them prestige and reputation. In the church of Christ, what matters most about true leadership is that leaders are willing to serve the needs of the people they lead, willing to be the least of all in their attitudes and demeanor. Their position of leadership is not to make them wealthier, more influential, more recognized, or more revered. On the contrary, self-effacement, modesty, and humility are key to true Christian leadership.

Tangibly, Jesus exemplified this kind of leadership when He stooped to wash the dirty feet of His disciples during the Last Supper (John 13:1–20). He took the position of a true servant and slave.

> So Christ expressed His love for His disciples. Their selfish spirit filled Him with sorrow, but He entered into no controversy with them regarding their difficulty. Instead He gave them an example they would never forget. His love for them was not easily disturbed or quenched. He knew that the Father had given all things into His hands, and that He came from God, and went to God. He had a full consciousness of His divinity; but He had laid aside His royal crown and kingly robes, and had taken the form of a servant. One of the last acts of His life on earth was to gird Himself as a servant, and perform a servant's part.[5]

What an incredible example for today's church leaders. Principles of good leadership apply in all forms of social organizations. But the leader in the church must be more than a leader, he or she must also be a servant. Arthur Keough astutely notes,

> There is an apparent contradiction between being a leader and being a servant. How can one lead and serve at the same time? Does not the leader occupy a position of honor? Does he not command and expect others to obey him? How, then, does he occupy the lower position of being a servant, of receiving order and fulfilling them?
>
> In order to resolve the paradox we must look at Jesus. He supremely represented the principle of leadership that serves. His whole life was one of service. And at the same time He was the greatest leader the world has ever seen.[6]

### Preserving church unity

In the New Testament various titles are used synonymously and interchangeably to refer to the leaders of local church communities: "pastor" (or "shepherd"), "teacher," "elder," and "overseer" (Ephesians 4:11; Titus 1:5, 7; 1 Peter 5:1–4). One of the primary responsibilities of these leadership positions is to preserve the unity of the church by safeguarding the purity of biblical teaching and carefully explaining the meaning of the Scriptures to the people (2 Timothy 2:15).

Paul saw this as a crucial responsibility of those who lead the church in the time of the end. "I charge you therefore before God and the Lord Jesus Christ, who will judge the living and the dead at His appearing and His kingdom: Preach the word! Be ready in season and out of season. Convince, rebuke, exhort, with all longsuffering and teaching. For the time will come when they will not endure sound doctrine, but according to their own desires, because they have itching ears, they will heap up for themselves teachers; and they will turn their ears away from the truth, and be turned aside to fables" (2 Timothy 4:1–4).

In writing to Timothy and Titus, Paul focused his thoughts

on the second coming of Jesus and on the day of judgment. The apostle uses all his fatherly authority to give Timothy his most important advice. In this context of the last days, with false teachings abounding and immorality rising, Timothy is to preach the Word of God. That is the ministry he has been called to. As Paul has already explained at the end of chapter 3, the Word of God is the most reliable source of teaching and moral guidance. Paul's encouragement goes on to express his desire that Timothy be ready to do his ministry in season and out of season, whether it is convenient or inconvenient. The gospel is always needed even though people may not realize it. As part of his teaching ministry, Timothy is to convince, rebuke, and exhort. These verbs are reminiscent of the guidance given by the Scriptures (2 Timothy 3:16). Clearly, Timothy's work is to follow, teach, and implement what he finds in the Scriptures with longsuffering and patience. Harsh and severe rebukes never bring a sinner to Christ.

Paul urged Titus to teach local elders to hold "fast the faithful word as he has been taught, that he may be able, by sound doctrine, both to exhort and convict those who contradict" (Titus 1:9). Beyond the responsibilities of a church leader to preserve the unity of the church, the leader is also charged with "equipping the saints," for "edifying the body of Christ, till we all come to the unity of the faith and of the knowledge of the Son of God" (Ephesians 4:12, 13).

### Church discipline

One of the main responsibilities of church organization is to deal with discipline. How discipline serves to preserve church unity is sometimes a sensitive subject and can be easily misunderstood. But from a biblical perspective church discipline centers on two important areas: preserving purity of doctrine and purity of life. As we have already seen, the New Testament maintains the importance of preserving the purity of biblical teaching in the wake of apostasy and false teaching, particularly at the end of time. The same goes for preserving the respectability of the community by guarding against immorality, dishonesty, and depravity. For this reason, the Scripture is spoken of as "profitable for doctrine, for reproof, for correction, for instruction in righteousness" (2 Timothy 3:16).

In Matthew 18:15–20 Jesus gave His disciples some principles regarding the discipline of those who are at fault. The Bible supports the concept of correction and accountability to each other in spiritual and moral matters. In fact, one of the distinguishing marks of the church is its holiness, or separation from the world (1 Corinthians 6:9–11; Ephesians 5:27). Scripture contains many examples of difficult situations that required the church to act decisively against immoral behaviors (1 Corinthians 5:1–5; Titus 1:10, 11; 2 John 7–11). Certain moral standards must be maintained for the sake of unity in a church community.

Reinder Bruinsma observes that the instruction to exercise discipline in Matthew 18 is situated between the parable of the lost sheep and the parable of the merciful servant; stories that highlight God's love for the lost and the golden rule of forgiveness. He further notes that, "One might sum it all up by saying that discipline can never be a mere legal action or only a political signal to the outside world that the church sets limits to what it allows. It can certainly never be vindictive or purely administrative. Those who administer discipline will always need to do so in humility, keenly aware of their own failings. Any sense of spiritual or moral superiority is misplaced."[7]

### Organizing for mission

Another important aspect of church leadership and church organization is mission, the communication of the good news of salvation. In Matthew 28:18–20, Jesus gave His disciples final instructions for their mission to the world. This Great Commission includes four key verbs: go, disciple, baptize, and teach. According to the Greek grammar of these verses, the main verb is to make disciples and the other three verbs indicate how this is accomplished. Disciples are made when believers go to all nations to preach the gospel, baptize people, and

117

teach them to observe what Jesus said.

As the church responds to this commission, God's kingdom is enlarged and more and more people of all nations join the ranks of those who accept Jesus as Savior. Their obedience to Jesus' command to be baptized and observe His teachings creates a new universal family. The new disciples are also assured of the presence of Jesus every day as they themselves make more disciples. The presence of Jesus is a promise of the presence of God. The gospel of Matthew begins with the announcement that the birth of Jesus is about "God with us" (Matthew 1:23) and ends with the promise of Jesus' continued presence until His second coming.

On the day of His ascension, Jesus also promised the coming of the Holy Spirit to give power to the church to accomplish this mission. "But you shall receive power when the Holy Spirit has come upon you; and you shall be witnesses to Me in Jerusalem, and in all Judea and Samaria, and to the end of the earth" (Acts 1:8).

In preparation for their mission to all nations, early Christian believers spent time in prayer. In Acts 1:14 and 2:46, the phrase "with one accord" also means "persevered with one mind." This came as a result of their being together in one place, seeking in prayer the fulfillment of Jesus' promise to send the Comforter.

> As the disciples waited for the fulfillment of the promise, they humbled their hearts in true repentance and confessed their unbelief. . . .
>
> The disciples prayed with intense earnestness for a fitness to meet men and in their daily intercourse to speak words that would lead sinners to Christ.[8]

The fellowship between the disciples and the intensity of their prayers prepared them for the momentous experience of Pentecost. As they drew nearer to God, the disciples were prepared by the Holy Spirit to become bold and fearless witnesses of Jesus' resurrection. This spiritual unity between them became the bedrock of their confidence for mission. This unity gave them a sense of community strength—each one of them could count on the support and courage of the others. Their unity and transformation of character made them different people. And, remarkably, leaders in Jerusalem took notice: "And they realized that they had been with Jesus" (Acts 4:13).

Good organization and wise leadership are essential to church unity. Christ is the head of the church, and the church prospers when church leaders embrace His example of leadership. Through the ministry of godly leaders, faithfulness to the Word, and consistent living, the gospel can be effectively shared with the entire world.

1. Richard Rice, *Reign of God: An Introduction to Christian Theology From a Seventh-day Adventist Perspective*, 2nd ed. (Berrien Springs, MI: Andrews University Press, 1997), 215.

2. In Matthew 16:18, Jesus used the Greek word *petra* to illustrate the solid foundation of the church in contrast to Peter, a mere human being. Both Peter and Paul understood this foundation to be only Jesus and also used the word *petra* when they identified Jesus as this rock (1 Peter 4:8; 1 Corinthians 10:4).

3. Ellen G. White, *The Desire of Ages* (Mountain View, CA: Pacific Press®,1940), 414.

4. Darius Jankiewicz, "Serving Like Jesus: Authority in God's Church," *Adventist Review*, March 13, 2014, 18.

5. White, *The Desire of Ages*, 644, 645.

6. G. Arthur Keough, *Our Church Today* (Nashville, TN: Review and Herald®, 1980), 106.

7. Reinder Bruinsma, *The Body of Christ: A Biblical Understanding of the Church* (Hagerstown, MD: Review and Herald®, 2009), 103, 104.

8. Ellen G. White, *The Acts of the Apostles* (Mountain View, CA: Pacific Press®, 1911), 36, 37.

13

# Final Restoration
# of Unity

One of the greatest promises of the Bible is Jesus' promise to come again. When He returns in the clouds of heaven, all that is earthly and human-made will be swept away. At the end of the millennium, this world with its wars, famines, diseases, and tragedies will become the dwelling place of the redeemed, finally reunited with their Lord and with one another. The new earth will be a place of righteousness and wholesomeness.

Hope in the second coming of Christ is a major theme of the New Testament, and for centuries Christians have longed for the fulfillment of this promise. This final chapter reviews this promise and what it means for Christian unity. The church, though often confronted with human limitations and weaknesses, longs for the moment when it is no longer challenged by fragmentation and lack of unity. What a glorious day it will be when the church is finally one with the Lord, reunited and restored in the earth made new.

### The certainty of Christ's return

Early Christians considered Christ's return "the blessed hope" (Titus 2:13). They expected all the prophecies and promises of Scripture to be fulfilled at His second advent. This was the great hope of their Christian pilgrimage. Today, all who love

Christ look forward to the day when they will be able to enjoy face-to-face fellowship with Him.

John 14:1–3 is the best-known promise of Jesus' second coming: "Let not your heart be troubled; you believe in God, believe also in Me. In My Father's house are many mansions; if it were not so, I would have told you. I go to prepare a place for you. And if I go and prepare a place for you, I will come again and receive you to Myself; that where I am, there you may be also." This promise describes life on the new earth as one of community and fellowship.

Christians believe in this promise because the Bible assures us of its fulfillment. We have this assurance because we believe in the words of Jesus, "I will come again" (verse 3). Just as Christ's first coming was prophesied, so His second coming is also foretold, even in the Old Testament. Before the Flood God told the patriarch Enoch that the Messiah's coming in glory would put an end to sin. He prophesied, "Behold, the Lord comes with ten thousand of His saints, to execute judgment on all, to convict all who are ungodly among them of all their ungodly deeds which they have committed in an ungodly way, and of all the harsh things which ungodly sinners have spoken against Him" (Jude 14, 15).

A thousand years before Jesus came to this earth, King David also prophesied of the Messiah's coming to gather God's people together:

Our God shall come, and shall not keep silent;
A fire shall devour before Him,
And it shall be very tempestuous all around Him.

He shall call to the heavens from above,
And to the earth, that He may judge His people:
"Gather My saints together to Me,
Those who have made a covenant with Me by sacri-
   fice" (Psalm 50:3–5).

The second coming of Jesus is closely linked to His first

advent. The prophecies that predicted His birth and ministry (e.g. Genesis 3:15; Micah 5:2; Isaiah 11:1; Daniel 9:25, 26) are the foundation for our hope and trust in the promises of His second coming. His first advent won the victory over Satan and redeemed humanity from sin and the forces of evil (Colossians 2:15). This victory at the cross is the promise of His ultimate victory over evil and sin. Christ "has appeared to put away sin by the sacrifice of Himself . . . [and] was offered once to bear the sins of many. To those who eagerly wait for Him He will appear a second time, apart from sin, for salvation" (Hebrews 9:26, 28).

### The promise of restoration

The Bible begins with the story of Earth's creation (Genesis 1, 2). It describes a beautiful and harmonious world entrusted to our first parents, Adam and Eve. It was perfect. The Bible's last two chapters mirror the perfection of the Genesis creation and speak of God creating a perfect and harmonious world for redeemed humanity (Revelation 21, 22). This time, however, it is more accurate to say re-creation, the restoration of the earth from the ravages of sin.

In many places, the Bible announces that the eternal home of the redeemed will be a real place, not an imaginary land. The redeemed will be able to see, hear, smell, touch, and feel a new experience, a new life. Isaiah 11:1–10 beautifully foretells the coming of the Messiah who will create this new era. He will eradicate all violence and usher in a new peace. The reign of God on this new earth will reestablish universal harmony.

One of the greatest joys the redeemed will experience on the new earth is the presence of God. He will dwell on the earth with the saints and, by virtue of the plan of salvation, enjoy the much anticipated reunion with humanity. At last, there will be no more sin, no more barriers between God and His friends. The relationship suspended in the Garden of Eden after the entrance of sin (Genesis 3:8, 22–24) will be fully restored on the new earth. This is the first step in the final restoration; harmony and unity will be reestablished in the entire universe.

### Resurrection and restored relationships

From the church's earliest days, the promise of Christ's return has, perhaps more than anything else, sustained the hearts of God's faithful people during times of trials. Whatever their struggles, whatever their inconsolable sorrows and pain, they had hope in Christ's return and all the wonderful promises associated with the Second Advent.

Christ's second coming will affect all humanity in profound ways. An important aspect of the establishment of God's kingdom is the gathering of the elect. "And He will send His angels with a great sound of a trumpet, and they will gather together His elect from the four winds, from one end of heaven to the other" (Matthew 24:31). At the moment of this gathering, the righteous dead will be resurrected and receive immortality (1 Corinthians 15:52, 53). The dead in Christ will rise first (1 Thessalonians 4:16). This is the moment so many have been waiting for. The resurrected righteous will reunite with those who have been longing for their presence and love. The diseased, aged, disfigured bodies that went down to the grave will be raised as new, immortal, perfect bodies, no longer marked by sin and decay. They will experience the completion of Christ's work of restoration, reflecting the perfect image of God intended at creation (Genesis 1:26; 1 Corinthians 15:46–49).

At the moment of Jesus' second advent, when the redeemed dead are resurrected, the righteous who are alive on earth will be changed and given new, perfect bodies. "For this corruptible must put on incorruption, and this mortal must put on immortality" (1 Corinthians 15:53). These two groups of the resurrected and transformed righteous "shall be caught up together . . . in the clouds to meet the Lord in the air. And thus we shall always be with the Lord" (1 Thessalonians 4:17).

### A new earth for the redeemed

"For behold, I create new heavens and a new earth; and the former shall not be remembered or come to mind" (Isaiah 65:17). Both Isaiah and John (Revelation 21:1) saw in vision the promised new earth. Among the many new things shown them in these visions, one of particular interest is the restoration of unity at the tree of life, which Adam lost because of his transgression (Genesis 3:22–24). Christ will restore this tree in the New Jerusalem, and access to it is one of the promises to those who overcome (Revelation 2:7). It could be that twelve kinds of fruit, a new kind each month, suggests a reason why Isaiah describes the new earth like this, " 'From one New Moon to another, and from one Sabbath to another, all flesh shall come to worship before Me,' says the LORD" (Isaiah 66:23). The reference to the "healing of the nations" in Revelation 22:2 also underscores God's intent to remove all barriers between people and restore humanity to its original purpose: one undivided family, living in harmony and peace, united in giving glory to God.

Ranko Stefanovic fittingly unpacks the meaning of this promise:

> "The healing of the nations" refers figuratively to the removal of all national and linguistic barriers and separation. . . . The leaves of the tree of life heal the breaches between nations. The nations are no longer "gentiles" but are united into one family as the true people of God (cf. [Rev.] 21:24-26). What Micah anticipated centuries earlier is now being fulfilled: "Nation will not lift up sword against nation, and never again will they train for war. Each of them will sit under his vine and under his fig tree, with no one to make them afraid" (Mic. 4:3-4; cf. Isa. 2:4). There on the banks of the river of life the redeemed will "invite his neighbor to sit" (Zech. 10) with him under the tree of life. The curing quality of the leaves of the tree will heal all wounds—racial, ethnic, tribal, or linguistic—that have torn and divided humanity for ages.[1]

### Life on the new earth

Two other prophecies of Isaiah tell of the great expectations the redeemed can anticipate in the new earth. In Isaiah 35:4–10, the renewed kingdom of God brings a total transformation of nature and a healing of diseases and sickness. Salvation results in joy and peace. Harmony is the new reality of God's kingdom. Several passages in Isaiah describe something new: "new things" (42:9; 48:6), "a new song" (42:10), "a new thing" (43:19), "a new name" (62:2). God will make all things new. Isaiah 65:21–25 also describes a new order. There is peace and harmony among all God's creatures. The covenant curses on the land for disobedience and rebellion (see Leviticus 26:14–17; Deuteronomy 28:30) will be canceled forever because sin is no more. Instead, there will be houses, food, and an abundance of blessings.

What will life be like in such a beautiful place? Some wonder, if after our bodies receive immortality and are fully restored into God's image, will we be able to recognize our friends and family? After Christ's resurrection, His disciples were able to recognize Him. Mary recognized His voice (John 20:11–16). Thomas recognized Jesus' physical appearance (verses 27, 28). The two disciples of Emmaus recognized His mannerisms (Luke 24:30, 31, 35). So if our bodies are to be similar to Jesus' resurrected body, we will certainly be able to recognize each other, and we can look forward to an eternity of restored relationships with one another. We can safely assume we will continue relationships with those we know and love.

"There the redeemed shall know, even as also they are known. The loves and sympathies which God Himself has planted in the soul shall there find truest and sweetest exercise. The pure communion with holy beings, the harmonious social life with the blessed angels and with the faithful ones of all ages who have washed their robes and made them white in the blood of the Lamb, the sacred ties that bind together 'the whole family in heaven and earth' (Ephesians 3:15)—these help to constitute the happiness of the redeemed."[2]

Paul's words to the Corinthians are a fitting conclusion: "Therefore, we do not lose heart. . . . For our light affliction, which is but for a moment, is working for us a far more exceeding and eternal weight of glory, while we do not look at the things which are seen, but at the things which are not seen. For the things which are seen are temporary, but the things which are not seen are eternal" (2 Corinthians 4:16–18).

The Bible speaks confidently of the moment when this earth will be re-created and the ravages of sin erased. At long last, humanity will be restored to its original purpose, and all people will live in harmony. Our current spiritual oneness will then be a living and eternal reality. This is our hope in Christ.

---

1. Ranko Stefanovic, *Revelation of Jesus Christ: Commentary on the Book of Revelation* (Berrien Springs, MI: Andrews University Press, 2002), 593.

2. Ellen G. White, *The Great Controversy* (Mountain View, CA: Pacific Press®, 1911), 677.